BLACK AMERICAN POETS
AND DRAMATISTS
OF THE HARLEM RENAISSANCE

Writers of English: Lives and Works

Black American Poets and Dramatists

OF THE HARLEM RENAISSANCE

Edited and with an Introduction by

Harold Bloom

CHELSEA HOUSE PUBLISHERS
New York   Philadelphia

Jacket illustration: Jacob Lawrence (b. 1917), *The Libraries Are Appreciated* (1943) (courtesy of the Philadelphia Museum of Art, The Louis E. Stern Collection).

CHELSEA HOUSE PUBLISHERS

Editorial Director Richard Rennert
Executive Managing Editor Karyn Gullen Browne
Picture Editor Adrian G. Allen
Copy Chief Robin James
Art Director Robert Mitchell
Manufacturing Director Gerald Levine

Writers of English: Lives and Works

Senior Editor S. T. Joshi
Series Design Rae Grant

Staff for BLACK AMERICAN POETS AND DRAMATISTS OF THE HARLEM RENAISSANCE

Assistant Editor Mary Sisson
Research Robert Green
Picture Researcher Matthew Dudley

3 5 7 9 8 6 4 2

Library of Congress Cataloging-in-Publication Data

Black American poets and dramatist of the Harlem Renaissance / edited and with an introduction by Harold Bloom.
     p.   cm.—(Writers of English)
     Includes bibliographical references.
     ISBN 0-7910-2207-2.—ISBN 0-7910-2232-3 (pbk.)
  1. American literature—Afro-American authors—History and criticism. 2. American literature—Afro-American authors—Bio-bibliography. 3. American literature—20th century—History and criticism. 4. American literature—20th century—Bio-bibliography. 5. Afro-Americans in literature. 6. Harlem Renaissance. I. Bloom, Harold. II. Series.
PS153.N5B5335 1994   94-5881
810.9'896073'09041—dc20   CIP
[B]

⊞ Contents

◈ User's Guide

THIS VOLUME PROVIDES biographical, critical, and bibliographical information on the ten most significant poets and dramatists of the Harlem Renaissance. Each chapter consists of three parts: a biography of the author, a selection of brief critical extracts about the author, and a bibliography of the author's published books.

The biography supplies a detailed outline of the important events in the author's life, including his or her major writings. The critical extracts are taken from a wide array of books and periodicals, from the author's lifetime to the present, and range in content from biographical to critical to historical. The extracts are arranged in chronological order by date of writing or publication, and a full bibliographical citation is provided at the end of each extract. Editorial additions or deletions are indicated within carets.

The author bibliographies list every separate publication—including books, pamphlets, broadsides, collaborations, and works edited or translated by the author—for works published in the author's lifetime; selected important posthumous publications are also listed. Titles are those of the first edition; if a work has subsequently come to be known under a variant title, this title is supplied within carets. In selected instances dates of revised editions are given where these are significant. Pseudonymous works are listed, but the pseudonyms under which these works were published are not. Periodicals edited by the author are listed only when the author has written most or all of the contents. Titles enclosed in square brackets are of doubtful authenticity. All works by the author, whether in English or in other languages, have been listed; English translations of foreign-language works are not listed unless the author has done the translation.

◈ *The Life of the Author*

Harold Bloom

NIETZSCHE, WITH EXULTANT ANGUISH, famously proclaimed that God was dead. Whatever the consequences of this for the ethical life, its ultimate literary effect certainly would have surprised the author Nietzsche. His French disciples, Foucault most prominent among them, developed the Nietzschean proclamation into the dogma that all authors, God included, were dead. The death of the author, which is no more than a Parisian trope, another metaphor for fashion's setting of skirt-lengths, is now accepted as literal truth by most of our current apostles of what should be called French Nietzsche, to distinguish it from the merely original Nietzsche. We also have French Freud or Lacan, which has little to do with the actual thought of Sigmund Freud, and even French Joyce, which interprets *Finnegans Wake* as the major work of Jacques Derrida. But all this is as nothing compared to the final triumph of the doctrine of the death of the author: French Shakespeare. That delicious absurdity is given us by the New Historicism, which blends Foucault and California fruit juice to give us the Word that Renaissance "social energies," and not William Shakespeare, composed *Hamlet* and *King Lear*. It seems a proper moment to murmur "enough" and to return to a study of the life of the author.

Sometimes it troubles me that there are so few masterpieces in the vast ocean of literary biography that stretches between James Boswell's great *Life* of Dr. Samuel Johnson and the late Richard Ellmann's wonderful *Oscar Wilde*. Literary biography is a crucial genre, and clearly a difficult one in which to excel. The actual nature of the lives of the poets seems to have little effect upon the quality of their biographies. Everything happened to Lord Byron and nothing at all to Wallace Stevens, and yet their biographers seem equally daunted by them. But even inadequate biographies of strong writers, or of weak ones, are of immense use. I have never read a literary biography from which I have not profited, a statement I cannot make about any other genre whatsoever. And when it comes to figures who are central to us—Dante, Shakespeare, Cervantes, Montaigne, Goethe, Whitman, Tolstoi, Freud, Joyce, Kafka among them—we reach out eagerly for every scrap that the biographers have gleaned. Concerning Dante and Shakespeare we know much too little, yet when we come to Goethe and Freud, where we seem to know more than everything, we still want to know more. The death of the author, despite our current resentniks, clearly was only a momentary fad. Something vital in every authentic lover of literature responds to Emerson's battle-cry sentence: "There is no history, only biography." Beyond that there is a deeper truth, difficult to come at and requiring a lifetime to understand, which is that there is no literature, only autobiography, however mediated, however veiled, however transformed. The events of Shakespeare's life included the composition of *Hamlet,* and that act of writing was itself a crucial act of living, though we do not yet know altogether how to read so doubled an act. When an author takes up a more overtly autobiographical stance, as so many do in their youth, again we still do not know precisely how to accommodate the vexed relation between life and work. T. S. Eliot, meditating upon James Joyce, made a classic statement as to such accommodation:

> We want to know who are the originals of his characters, and what were
> the origins of his episodes, so that we may unravel the web of memory
> and invention and discover how far and in what ways the crude material
> has been transformed.

When a writer is not even covertly autobiographical, the web of memory and invention is still there, but so subtly woven that we may never unravel it. And yet we want deeply never to stop trying, and not merely because we are curious, but because each of us is caught in her own network of memory and invention. We do not always recall our inventions, and long before we age we cease to be certain of the extent to which we have invented our memories. Perhaps one motive for reading is our need to unravel our own webs. If our masters could make, from their lives, what we read, then we can be moved by them to ask: What have we made or lived in relation to what we have read? The answers may be sad, or confused, but the question is likely, implicitly, to go on being asked as long as we read. In Freudian terms, we are asking: What is it that we have repressed? What have we forgotten, unconsciously but purposively: What is it that we flee? Art, literature necessarily included, is regression in the service of the ego, according to a famous Freudian formula. I doubt the Freudian wisdom here, but indubitably it is profoundly suggestive. When we read, something in us keeps asking the equivalent of the Freudian questions: From what or whom is the author in flight, and to what earlier stages in her life is she returning, and why?

Reading, whether as an art or a pastime, has been damaged by the visual media, television in particular, and might be in some danger of extinction in the age of the computer, except that the psychic need for it continues to endure, presumably because it alone can assuage a central loneliness in elitist society. Despite all sophisticated or resentful denials, the reading of imaginative literature remains a quest to overcome the isolation of the individual consciousness. We can read for information, or entertainment, or for love of the language, but in the end we seek, in the author, the person whom we have not found, whether in ourselves or in others. In that quest, there always are elements at once aggressive and defensive, so that reading, even in childhood, is rarely free of hidden anxieties. And yet it remains one of the few activities not contaminated by an entropy of spirit. We read in hope, because we lack companionship, and the author can become the object of the most idealistic elements in our search for the wit and inventiveness we so desperately require. We read biography, not as a supplement to reading the author, but as a second, fresh attempt to understand what always seems to evade us in the work, our drive towards a kind of identity with the author.

This will-to-identity, though recently much deprecated, is a prime basis for the experience of sublimity in reading. *Hamlet* retains its unique position in the Western canon not because most readers and playgoers identify themselves with the prince, who clearly is beyond them, but rather because they find themselves again in the power of the language that represents him with such immediacy and force. Yet we know that neither language nor social energy created Hamlet. Our curiosity about Shakespeare is endless, and never will be appeased. That curiosity itself is a value, and cannot be separated from the value of *Hamlet* the tragedy, or Hamlet the literary character. It provokes us that Shakespeare the man seems so unknowable, at once everyone and no one as Borges shrewdly observes. Critics keep telling us otherwise, yet something valid in us keeps believing that we would know Hamlet better if Shakespeare's life were as fully known as the lives of Goethe and Freud, Byron and Oscar Wilde, or best of all, Dr. Samuel Johnson. Shakespeare never will have his Boswell, and Dante never will have his Richard Ellmann. How much one would give for a detailed and candid *Life of Dante* by Petrarch, or an outspoken memoir of Shakespeare by Ben Jonson! Or, in the age just past, how superb would be rival studies of one another by Hemingway and Scott Fitzgerald! But the list is endless: think of *Oscar Wilde* by Lord Alfred Douglas, or a joint biography of Shelley by Mary Godwin, Emilia Viviani, and Jane Williams. More than our insatiable desire for scandal would be satisfied. The literary rivals and the lovers of the great writers possessed perspectives we will never enjoy, and without those perspectives we dwell in some poverty in regard to the writers with whom we ourselves never can be done.

There is a sense in which imaginative literature *is* perspectivism, so that the reader is likely to be overwhelmed by the work's difficulty unless its multiple perspectives are mastered. Literary biography matters most because it is a storehouse of perspectives, frequently far surpassing any that are grasped by the particular biographer. There are relations between authors' lives and their works of kinds we have yet to discover, because our analytical instruments are not yet advanced enough to perform the necessary labor. Perhaps a novel, poem, or play is not so much a regression in the service of the ego, as it is an amalgam of *all* the Freudian mechanisms of defense, all working together for the apotheosis of the ego. Freud valued art highly, but thought that the aesthetic enterprise was no rival for psychoanalysis, unlike religion and philosophy. Clearly Freud was mistaken; his own anxieties about his indebtedness to Shakespeare helped produce the weirdness of his joining in the lunacy that argued for the Earl of Oxford as the author of Shakespeare's plays. It was Shakespeare, and not "the poets," who was there before Freud arrived at his depth psychology, and it is Shakespeare who is there still, well out ahead of psychoanalysis. We see what Freud would not see, that psychoanalysis is Shakespeare prosified and systematized. Freud is part of literature, not of "science," and the biography of Freud has the same relations to psychoanalysis as the biography of Shakespeare has to *Hamlet* and *King Lear,* if only we knew more of the life of Shakespeare.

Western literature, particularly since Shakespeare, is marked by the representation of internalized change in its characters. A literature of the ever-growing inner self is in itself a large form of biography, even though this is the biography of imaginary beings, from Hamlet to the sometimes nameless protagonists of Kafka and Beckett. Skeptics might want to argue that all literary biography concerns imaginary beings, since authors make themselves up, and every biographer gives us a creation curiously different from the same author as seen by the writer of a rival *Life.* Boswell's Johnson is not quite anyone else's Johnson, though it is now very difficult for us to disentangle the great Doctor from his gifted Scottish friend and follower. The life of the author is not merely a metaphor or a fiction, as is "the Death of the Author," but it always does contain metaphorical or fictive elements. Those elements are a part of the value of literary biography, but not the largest or the crucial part, which is the separation of the mask from the man or woman who hid behind it. James Joyce and Samuel Beckett, master and sometime disciple, were both of them enigmatic personalities, and their biographers have not, as yet, fully expounded the mystery of these contrasting natures. Beckett seems very nearly to have been a secular saint: personally disinterested, heroic in the French Resistance, as humane a person ever to have composed major fictions and dramas. Joyce, self-obsessed even as Beckett was preternaturally selfless, was the Milton of the twentieth century. Beckett was perhaps the least egoistic post-Joycean, post-Proustian, post-Kafkan of writers. Does that illuminate the problematical nature of his work, or does it simply constitute another problem? Whatever the cause, the question matters. The only death of the author that is other than literal, and that matters, is the fate only of weak writers. The strong, who become canonical, never die, which is what the canon truly is about. To be read forever is the Life of the Author.

 *Introduction*

COUNTEE CULLEN, introducing his anthology, *Caroling Dusk* (1927), said of the African-American poets of the Twenties that "theirs is also the heritage of the English language." "Rhymed polemics," he added, did not typify his poets, who went back to Paul Laurence Dunbar (1872–1906) and then included James Weldon Johnson, Claude McKay, Sterling Brown, Langston Hughes, Cullen himself, and Jean Toomer, the principal poets now generally assigned to the Harlem Renaissance. McKay, Brown, Hughes, Cullen, and Toomer hardly constituted a school, though they help to mark off an era. Except for Toomer, these poets had more in common with John Keats than with Ezra Pound and T. S. Eliot: their blackness insulated them against literary Modernism, which may have been all to the good. Langston Hughes, on internal evidence, was stimulated by Carl Sandburg, now forgotten as a poet but useful in helping to focus Hughes's polemic on behalf of his people. Like his fellow poets of the Harlem Renaissance, Hughes shrewdly found his models in poets a little remote from him in time and place. Only in the generation prefigured by Melvin B. Tolson, and culminating in Robert Hayden and in Gwendolyn Brooks, is there much of a direct influx of the High Modernism of Eliot and of Hart Crane, and by then enough of a black poetic tradition had been forged so that the influence could be accommodated, most brilliantly by the Hayden of "Middle Passage," "Runagate Runagate," and such ballads as those of "Remembrance" and "Nat Turner."

There are powerfully shaped poems in Claude McKay's work, where the mode of insulation is heightened by culture, and by the penitence of his turn to Roman Catholicism. His devotional sonnets seem to me stronger than most critics now acknowledge, and are scarcely fashionable, yet their highly wrought baroque inten-sity will preserve them into a time more receptive to formal control than our own. Countee Cullen already seems undervalued, as does Edwin Arlington Robinson, who mediated Keats for Cullen (on the basis again of internal evidence). Like Robinson, Cullen tones down his cadences to a perpetually dying fall, perfectly expressive not only of a sense of belatedness, as in Robinson, but also of a disciplined sensibility attempting an impossible balance between moral outrage and the realiza-tion that such outrage in itself cannot constitute a poem. Like Oscar Wilde, and like E. A. Robinson, Cullen knew that all bad poetry is sincere, and he had a passionate conviction that he must not add to the mass of bad poetry. He saw himself not as a black Keats but as a black poet who had identified Keats both with nature and with poetry. At our confused moment, Keats is held by many to be irrelevant to an African-American poet, but Cullen prophesied against such a limitation in his "To Certain Critics":

> No radical option narrows grief,
> Pain is no patriot,
> And sorrow plaits her dismal leaf
> For all as lief as not.

The play on "leaf" and "lief," a melancholy poetic pun, is characteristic of Cullen, whose wry nobility of stance rarely faltered. Like McKay, Cullen may return in favor after the politically correct Millennium that approaches an angelic America. Impressive as Langston Hughes's exemplary career was, his actual poems rarely go beyond the rough populism of Sandburg's *The People, Yes*. Few poets have been more consistently sincere in their poems than Hughes, and his selfless love for his people is morally powerful. But—unlike McKay and Cullen at their best—Hughes gave all his heart to prophecy, and little of his care to working out an adequate form. Sterling Brown wavered between the Milton-Keats mode of McKay and Cullen and the Sandburgian rhetoric of Hughes, finally evolving into more of the latter. It may be that Jean Toomer's *Cane* (1923) will be seen eventually as the poetic masterpiece of the Harlem Renaissance. Anything but an ideologue, Toomer is a strange, later flowering of what needs to be called black pastoral, and his lyrical intensity sometimes suggests the heightened incantatory style of his friend Hart Crane. The best poem in Cullen's *Caroling Dusk* seems to me Toomer's "November Cotton Flower," with its magical vision of a time of natural epiphany:

> . . . the branch, so pinched and slow,
> Failed in its function as the autumn rake;
> Drouth fighting soil had caused the soil to take
> All water from the streams; dead birds were found
> In wells a hundred feet below the ground—
> Such was the season when the flower bloomed.

Toomer is the authentic link between Dunbar and the African-American poets of highest achievement: Robert Hayden and Jay Wright, Rita Dove and Thylias Moss. Protest and politics will wane as economic justice gains; someday perhaps black poets will be free for purely poetic struggles.

—H. B.

Arna Bontemps
1902–1973

ARNAUD WENDELL BONTEMPS was born on October 13, 1902, in Alexandria, Louisiana, to Paul Bismark and Maria Carolina Pembroke Bontemps. When Arna was three, his family moved to Los Angeles after encountering racist incidents. Mrs. Bontemps was a schoolteacher and greatly encouraged Arna's love for books and learning until her death in 1915. To the disappointment of his father, Arna's literary interests led him away from the traditional family trade of brick masonry. Between 1917 and 1920 he attended San Fernando Academy, a white boarding school, and, upon graduation, entered Pacific Union College in Angwin, California, from which he graduated in 1923.

Bontemps, who resented much of his formal education as devoid of recognition of the achievements of fellow blacks, guarded against losing contact with black society and the rich cadences of Creole and black dialects. Bontemps's literary career began in 1924 with the publication of one of his poems in the *Crisis*. In the same year he moved to New York to take a teaching position at the Harlem Academy. Bontemps's poetry won him *Opportunity* magazine's Alexander Pushkin Poetry Prize in 1926 and 1927. During his short stay in Harlem, Bontemps married Alberta Johnson (in 1926) and found friends among the Harlem Renaissance writers and white literati from other parts of New York. Bontemps shared with the Harlem writers an atavistic longing for African traditions and was greatly influenced by Langston Hughes, who also became a great friend of his, and Countee Cullen, among others.

Bontemps's first novel, *God Sends Sunday*, was published in 1931. Set within the black sporting world, the book has been highly praised for Bontemps's economical and poetic use of language as well as his ability to capture the rhythmic cadences of black dialect. In 1939 Bontemps collaborated with Countee Cullen on adapting the novel for the stage.

After resigning from the Harlem Academy in 1931, Bontemps moved to Huntsville, Alabama, to teach at Oakwood Junior College. *Opportunity* awarded him the 1932 literary prize for his short story "A Summer Tragedy." In Alabama Bontemps began writing juvenile literature, partly in the hope of presenting a positive image of blacks in America. His first children's book, *Popo and Fifina* (1932), written in collaboration with Langston Hughes, follows the adventures of two children in rural Haiti. In 1934 *You Can't Pet a Possum* appeared. Bontemps wrote many other works for children, including *We Have Tomorrow* (1945), *Slappy Hooper, the Wonderful Sign Painter* (1946), and *Mr. Kelso's Lion* (1970). He also wrote two biographical works for young adults on the abolitionist Frederick Douglass—*Frederick Douglass: Slave, Fighter, Freeman* (1959) and *Free at Last: The Life of Frederick Douglass* (1971)—as well as a young adult biography of Booker T. Washington, *Young Booker: Booker T. Washington's Early Days* (1972).

In 1934 Bontemps resigned his position at Oakwood Junior College. The next year he accepted a teaching position at Shiloh Academy and moved to Chicago. He resigned from Shiloh Academy in 1937 to add his talents to the Illinois Writers' Project. In 1936 Bontemps published *Black Thunder*, which proved to be his most celebrated work. The novel is set in the historical context of a slave insurrection in 1800 in Henrico County, Virginia, and draws much from early slave narratives. *Black Thunder* was praised for its uninhibited retelling of the black revolutionary sentiment brewing in the slave states of early America, but it was Bontemps's powerful use of language, especially dialect, that brought the novel its critical acclaim.

In 1938 Bontemps gave up teaching in order to write full-time. He accepted the Rosenwald Fellowship and set out for the Caribbean. His travels resulted in *Drums at Dusk* (1939), a depiction of a Haitian slave revolt around the time of the French Revolution. The book was disparaged by some reviewers for its romantic landscape painting and weak narrative structure. In 1943 Bontemps completed his masters of library science at the University of Chicago and became librarian at Fisk University in Nashville, Tennessee, a position that he held until 1965. He devoted his energies to enlarging the library's collection of black American literature and anthologizing black American writings and folklore in such volumes as *Golden Slippers: An Anthology of Negro Poetry for Young Readers* (1941), *American Negro Poetry* (1963; rev. 1974), *Great Slave Narratives* (1969), and *The Harlem Renaissance Remembered* (1972), which contributed much to the history of black American literary achievement. The slim poetry collection *Personals*, published in London in 1963, gathers together the verse he had written over his entire literary career. Arna Bontemps died on June 4, 1973, in Nashville, Tennessee.

▣ *Critical Extracts*

IONE MORRISON RIDER   In 1935 the young author brought his wife and three young children to visit in Los Angeles. We of a small branch of the Los Angeles Public Library remember a man of quiet aspect and sensitive features applying for a borrower's card. His backhand signature had an almost feminine spidery grace. Where had we seen that name before? One of the staff suddenly realized that it was on a book on our shelves— on two of them. *God Sends Sunday* happened to be in. We asked the quiet reader, was it his? It was, he answered with a slight smile.

Thereafter he came almost daily to read. We looked forward to learning his opinions on this or that new book, in brief intervals between desk and reference demands. He kept in touch with the best current writing, and although reticent shared his views generously when asked.

During this interval he watched over his children's reading, and continued his study of the simplification of dialect. He read and analyzed children's books suggested by our children's librarian, and showed keen interest in teaching methods in neighborhood schools. He came to talk to children at the library story hour—a weekly event held, because of the lack of a separate room, right in the children's room with the hubbub of the charging desk just beyond. The gentle artist must have been shocked within himself to find waiting, not the usual fifty, but about two hundred urchins of different races, including Mexican, Negro, Japanese. They surged in waves around him on the clean linoleum floor. He had to pick his way between grimy hands and bare feet to the corner from which he told the story of Toussaint L'Ouverture and read aloud several of Langston Hughes's poems.

Then came the evening when Mr. Bontemps brought in Langston Hughes, en route from Mexico. Mr. Hughes is a charming citizen of the world; sophisticated, poised. He looked with interest over our collection of books, spoke of liking Helen Sewell's drawings for *The Dream Keeper*, was amused to learn that his adult books are stolen here as they are in other libraries. He's happiest, he mentioned, among people of the theater. Among artists there is no such thing as race-consciousness; there is only art-consciousness. Nevertheless, it is evident that he is dedicated to conscious expression as a Negro. ⟨. . .⟩

For some time Mr. Bontemps has been working on an adventure story for older boys, with a Caribbean background. He also has under way another historical novel, which is concerned with Haiti. Twice recently he has revisited that fascinating island. "No one," he wrote recently from there, "has yet done this island justice. It is too heavy with color. One must *see* the flamboyant tree in flower, or he will never know."

True, beyond a doubt. Yet we venture to hope that through the seeing of such artists as Arna Bontemps we also may feel its magic, gain some measure of understanding of its proud people. Whatever is yet to come from his pen we await with anticipation, confident that it will be poetically conceived, and written with distinction.

Ione Morrison Rider, "Arna Bontemps," *Horn Book* 15, No. 1 (January–February 1939): 17, 19

ARNA BONTEMPS   No, there was something special about being young and a poet in Harlem in the middle 'twenties. We couldn't quite explain it, but one of our advocates on Park Avenue made an interesting suggestion. Primitive man, she said, had contacts with the infinite which civilization has broken. Primitive man was sharper, more acute in his intuition. Relying always on logic and reason, civilized man has lost the one thing most essential. In America the Indian and the Negro are nearer to the unspoiled primitive than are other people. The Indian's spirit is crushed. The Negro—well, see for yourself!

Up and down the streets of Harlem untamed youngsters were doing a wild dance called the Charleston. They were flitting over the sidewalks like mad while their companions, squatting nearby, beat out tom-tom rhythms on kitchenware. The unsuspecting stranger who paused to observe the performance was in danger of being surrounded, shoved into their circle and compelled to attempt a camel walk.

At parties, in ballrooms and on neighborhood stages the older people proved that age, or the lack of it, had nothing to do with this joy, this abandon, this . . . primitivism. They proved it, too, at house rent parties where they drank bathtub gin, ate pig's knuckles and danced with the lights off.

> Darkness brings the jungle to our rooms . . .
> darkness hangs our room with pendulums
> of vine . . .

The link with the jungle was obvious. In the little house-front churches there was swaying and moaning and shouting. Wasn't that proof? On a voodoo island such behavior would be called 'possession'. Would it be any more real or complete than this? No, the American Negro, our friend insisted, was not quite civilized—fortunately. In his play and in his worship his wildness was still apparent. In his work and in his art it had almost disappeared.

The 'New Negro' was to recapture this definite, though sometimes dim, quality in poetry, painting and song. By this means he must transmit it to all America. Through us, no less, America would regain a certain value that civilization had destroyed.

The idea intoxicated us. We went to work zealously, and some Americans saw the things we did. And the miracle of the whole notion was that it came so near to taking root. Our group came within an inch of giving America, if not as much as our friend from Park Avenue had hoped, at least a certain new aesthetic value. It came close to repeating in the United States, say, what the Pre-Raphaelite Brotherhood had done in England two generations or so earlier. ⟨. . .⟩

The young intellectuals who came to Harlem in the middle of the 'twenties made a wonderful discovery. They found that it is fun to be a Negro under some conditions. Those who, like myself, had grown up in mixed or predominately white communities even found that some segregation can be fun, when it's completely voluntary. But the 'New Negroes' had lived long enough to learn that it is never fun to be an alien. It is neither pleasant nor wholesome to be deprived of the freedom of movement or of friendship or of participation in the essential life of one's country.

Harlem must go. The American bloodstream cannot manage hard clots of such size and density. All the other little Harlems must change. Otherwise America will be balkanized into a nation of mutually incompatible minorities. For the ideas and plans and the vigilance and distrust necessary to hem Harlem in and to keep it there, will create other Harlems, and all of them will not be black . . .

Arna Bontemps, "Preface," *Personals* (London: Paul Breman, 1963), pp. 6–8, 11

JOHN O'BRIEN   INTERVIEWER: Both your fiction and your poetry are concerned with themes of history and time. You use the image of the pendulum rather than the river to describe your sense of history.

BONTEMPS: That impressed me a long time ago and I still feel that history is a pendulum that does recur. But in each recurrence there is a difference.

INTERVIEWER: And the image of the river would suggest a sense of completion?

BONTEMPS: That's right. The river is finished, it goes to its outlet. I don't think the river is a very good metaphor for time because we live in a universe that is perpetually revolving. And in our own experience we always arrive at the same point again, but when we get there we find that time has worked some changes in us.

INTERVIEWER: Do you think that in your poetry you look toward the past with a desire to recapture it?

BONTEMPS: Well, there certainly is some nostalgia. I don't know whether I was conciously yearning for the past. I don't think I could ever recapture the past. I had a yearning for something, something in my own life. Unlike most black writers I yearned for something in my past because I had something there that I could look upon with a certain amount of longing. A great many writers whom I have known have wanted to forget their pasts.

INTERVIEWER: In the preface to *Personals* you suggest that much of the writing of the Renaissance looked backward and tried to establish a link with the jungle.

BONTEMPS: It has impressed me in black literature that the primitive is often superior to the civilized or educated man.

INTERVIEWER: Of course, in the white Western mind the primitive is usually associated with disorder and perhaps violence. Many black writers seem to see it as a way of tapping some resource in man that frees him from the tyrannical norms of the existing rationalistic culture.

BONTEMPS: That's right. Spontaneity seems quite important in the black culture. The person who can act with spontaneity is the one favored by nature. One of the things I talked about a great deal when I taught at Yale was that Primitivism is often thought of as having no rationale to it. In fact, oftentimes it was actually the result of a long development that had been experimented with and proved. Some African tribes that had no written language—tribes we would take to be the more primitive ones—

sometimes had the most sophisticated art. The bronzes of Benin in Nigeria which had such a great influence on modern painters like Picasso, were the work of a tribe that never had a written language. And a tribe in Eastern Africa which has given so many collections of proverbs to us had no written language either until very recently. I have deduced from this that they had some reason for not writing down their language, not that they were incapable. They were capable of things that go deeper than merely writing a language. It was a conscious choice of theirs. So I toyed with the thought that they deliberately refrained from developing written records. Because of the nature of their life, which was very fluid, it may be that tribes that had written languages were more vulnerable. This might be part of their defense against invasion and oppression. In other words, they must have very carefully considered the disadvantages of writing. There certainly were languages in Africa long before there were Western languages. These languages existed not only in Egypt but down into mid-Africa, into that area in Rhodesia where cities were buried whose languages are known. So, I think the "book" is something they all knew about, talked about, rejected.

John O'Brien, *Interviews with Black Writers* (New York: Liveright, 1973), pp. 13–15

JACK CONROY   It has now been more than a year since Arna, my cherished friend and esteemed colleague for such a long period, died. On June 4, 1973, to be exact. I recently looked through the small volume of his verse, *Personals*, published by Paul Breman in London in 1963, and realized that it will soon be half a century since Arna, a wide-eyed young poet fresh out of college, arrived in New York City from California. His first impressions—expressed in more detail in his memoir which introduces *The Harlem Renaissance Remembered* (Dodd, Mead, 1972), a collection of essays he edited—are set down in the preface to *Personals*:

> In some places the autumn of 1924 may have been an
> unremarkable season. In Harlem it was like a foretaste of paradise.
> A blue haze descended at night and with it strings of fairy lights
> on the broad avenues. From the window of a small room in an
> apartment on Fifth and 129th Street I looked over the rooftops of
> Negrodom and tried to believe my eyes. What a city! What a
> world!
>   And what a city for a colored boy to be leaving home for the
> first time! Twenty-one, sixteen months out of college, full of

> golden hopes and romantic dreams, I had come all the way from
> Los Angeles to find the job I wanted, to hear the music of my
> taste, to see serious plays and, God willing, to become a writer.

The Negro Renaissance was beginning to build up a full head of steam, and young Bontemps was soon an active participant. He was able to find some teaching assignments in private schools while continuing his studies, and during that first year in Harlem he had his first poem accepted for publication in *The Crisis*, then edited by W. E. B. Du Bois. It was indeed a good year for the young poet, as was 1926 when he won his first poetry prize and took unto himself a wife. Somehow, Harlem remained a pleasant and exhilarating haven during the twenties, though racial disturbances erupted in other American cities. "Spared these convulsions," Bontemps notes, "New York became a locus for what I would regard as a more exciting and perhaps more telling assault on oppression than the dreary blood-in-the-streets strategy of preceding years."

This statement, it seems to me, provides a clue to Arna's creative method, which often evoked a more poignant emotional response by quiet eloquence than a more violent and hortatory approach might have accomplished. ⟨. . .⟩

Looking through the copy of *Personals* Arna inscribed for me ("to Jack, these vestiges of the Twenties"), I thought as I read such selections as "Southern Mansion," "To a Young Girl Leaving the Hill Country," and "A Black Man Talks of Reaping" that Arna had never lost that precious sense of wonder and discovery that flooded him when he first beheld Harlem. There is the elegiac and nostalgic note that pervades much of his later work, both in prose and verse, and makes it so appealing and heart-warming.

Jack Conroy, "Memories of Arna Bontemps: Friend and Collaborator," *American Libraries* 5, No. 11 (December 1974): 605–6

ARTHUR P. DAVIS   Bontemps' poems make use of several recurring themes: the alien-and-exile allusions so often found in New Negro poetry; strong racial suggestiveness and applications; religious themes and imagery subtly used; and the theme of return to a former time, a former love, or a remembered place. On occasion he combines in a way common to lyrical writing the personal with the racial or the general. Many of these poems are protest poems; but the protest is oblique and suggestive rather than frontal. Over all of Bontemps' poetry there is a sad, brooding quality, a sombre "Il Penseroso" meditative cast. In *Personals* there are no obviously joyous or humorous pieces.

The most popular theme in these verses is that of return. There are seven poems dealing in some way with this subject. The one entitled "Return" has a double thrust, the coming back to an old love takes an atavistic coloring: "Darkness brings the jungle to our room: / the throb of rain is the throb of muffled drums. / . . . This is a night of love / retained from those lost nights our fathers slept in huts." There is definitely here the kind of alien-and-exile comparison found in these New Negro poems; the highest joy the lovers (real or imagined) can have is the remembered ancestral love in an idyllic Africa.

In a different way, "Southen Mansion" is also a return poem because for the speaker "The years go back with an iron clank. . . ." Two waves of remembered sound come to him: music from the house and the clank of chains in the cotton field. Because of the latter, only ghosts and the poplars "standing there still as death" and symbolizing death—only they—remain.

"To a Young Girl Leaving the Hill Country" is a return poem with a Wordsworthian slant. The speaker tells the girl that she has ignored the hills of her native place, and she will therefore come back a bent old lady "to seek the girl she was in those familiar stones." He continues: "then perhaps you'll understand / just how it was you drew from them and they from you." For Bontemps, one seemingly finds his identity return to his remembered past.

"Prodigal" speaks of returning to old scenes with more understanding: "I shall come back knowing / the old unanswered questions on your mouth." "Idolatry" tells of a return to a dead love: "For I will build a chapel in the place / where our love died and I will journey there. . . ." In the poem "Lancelot" the knight himself comes back after many years: "It is long, so long since I was here, Elaine, / . . . you did not think that I would come again. . . ."

What is this concern with the past—with old loves, old places, ghosts of yesterday? Is there for Bontemps, as for Boswell, greater joy in the backward glance than in the living experience? Is he simply a late romanticist with a yen "For old unhappy far-off things, / And battles long ago"? The answer is not evident in these poems. Perhaps the answer is what each reader finds them.

Arthur P. Davis, *From the Dark Tower: Afro-American Writers 1900 to 1960* (Washington, DC: Howard University Press, 1974), pp. 85–86

ROBERT BONE   In a little-noticed but important essay which appeared in 1950, Arna Bontemps discusses the demise of the Harlem Renaissance. "The Depression," he asserts, "put an end to the dream world of renaissance Harlem . . ." ("Famous WPA Authors," *Negro Digest,* June 1950). Yet even as he laments the passing of those exciting years, he celebrates the advent of a second literary awakening, "less gaudy but closer to realities" than the first. He associates this new development with the Federal Writers Projects of the 1930's, and more precisely with the Illinois Project, whose headquarters were located in the city of Chicago.

Bontemps was himself a firsthand witness of these events. Having left Alabama in the fall of 1933, he spent almost two years with his relatives in Watts before moving on to Chicago. There he enrolled at the university as a graduate student of English in the fall of 1935. Before many months had passed, he made the acquaintance of Richard Wright, and through him, the South Side Writers Group, whose membership included such aspiring authors as poet Margaret Walker and playwright Theodore Ward. Founded by Wright in April of 1936, this group offered mutual criticism and moral support to young black writers within the framework of a Marxist ideology. ⟨. . .⟩

Under the influence of these associations, Bontemps' writing took a turn to the left. If we examine his work prior to 1935—his early verse, his first novel, *God Sends Sunday* (1931), and his Alabama tales—we find a sensibility molded by the themes and forms of the Harlem Renaissance. After 1935, however, Bontemps accommodates to the new revolutionary mood. His second novel, *Black Thunder* (1936), depicts the slave rebellion led by Gabriel Prosser, while his third, *Drums at Dusk* (1939), is concerned with the Haitian insurrection whose leader was Toussaint L'Ouverture. ⟨. . .⟩

This alteration in the mythic content of black writing signals the emergence of a new literary generation. From the perspective of 1950, Bontemps tries to define the relationship of the Wright generation to his own: "Obviously the new talents come in schools or waves. Either the writing impulse spreads by a sort of chain reaction or given conditions stimulate all who are exposed to them. One way or the other, Harlem got its renaissance in the middle twenties, centering around the *Opportunity* contests and Fifth Avenue Awards Dinners. Ten years later Chicago reenacted it on WPA without finger bowls but with increased power."

The clear implication is that Chicago, no less than Harlem, was the site of a cultural awakening. If Bontemps is correct, literary historians should be thinking in terms of a Chicago Renaissance. The issues are complex, for variables both of space and time are involved. The torch was passing not only from Harlem to Chicago, but from one generation to the next. Not all of the important work of the Wright generation was accomplished in the city of Chicago, but the new movement clearly had its focus there.

Robert Bone, "Arna Bontemps," *Down Home: A History of Afro-American Short Fiction from Its Beginnings to the End of the Harlem Renaissance* (New York: G. P. Putnam's Sons, 1975), pp. 284–86

EUGENE B. REDMOND   Between 1924 and 1931 Bontemps's poems were published widely in various magazines and periodicals and he won poetry prizes from both *The Crisis* and *Opportunity*. His only published volume of poetry, *Personals,* did not come out until 1963 (Paul Bremen).

Personals is a personal statement that sums up much of Bontemps's poetry. For throughout the book there is the use of "I" or "we" or "us." His poetry is personal, like Robert Hayden's, Countee Cullen's and Frank Horne's. A comfortableness also attends Bontemps's poetry—not a smug comfort, but the comfort of stability and careful workmanship. He was among those poets who, unlike Dunbar, had the security of college degrees and access to books unlimited. Consequently there is little of the yearning for instant recognition or the overanxiety that the anticipation of fame creates. Bontemps writes of love ("love's brown arms"), the African past ("The Return" and "Nocturne at Bethesda"), defiance and strength ("Close Your Eyes"). Reminiscent of Toomer's "Reapers," "A Black Man Talks of Reaping" surveys the sturdy, dependable tradition of black labor and concludes that the laborers' children "feed on bitter fruit." Billie Holiday would later reflect on a hanging in the South and write "Strange Fruit." And we recall that since James Whitfield, black poets have pointed to the contradictions in American Christianity and the barren-versus-bearing theme.

Bontemps also followed the Harlem Renaissance pattern of romanticizing a pagan Afro-American or African. With the taste of slavery and the dialect tradition still bitter on their tongues, these poets leaped backwards over slavery to another place and another clime. Bontemps does just this in "The Return," which closely resembles Cullen's "Heritage" and some of the atavistic pieces of Hughes and McKay. Bontemps speaks of "remembered rain," "the friendly ghost," "lost nights," "dance of rain," "jungle sky," "muffled drums," and then suggests:

> Let us go back into the dusk again. . . .

Dusk, ebony, jet, night, evenings, purple, blue, raven, and other such synonyms for Blacks are frequently employed to great effect and power by Afro-American poets. Likewise symbols or images of invisibility and blindness are also prevalent in black writing. Bontemps employs and implies such states in several poems in which he achieves a surreal quality—a dreamlike longing for another time and another place (again, a pattern in the poetry of the period). If you "Close Your Eyes," Bontemps says, you can go back to what you were, and maybe the song, as with Toomer, will "in time return to thee." Closing the eyes will also allow one to "walk bravely enough." Away from the daily limelight and without the constant pressure (cf. Cullen) to succeed and hold up the light of the race, Bontemps developed strong statements using conventional poetic patterns with occasional free-verse experimentation. Personal and powerful, Bontemps's poetry looks ahead to a similar stamina (this time in a new dialect) exhibited by Sterling Brown in *Southern Road*. For even though Bontemps tells us, in "Golgotha Is a Mountain,"

> One day I will crumble,

we know that the dust will fossilize and "make a mountain":

> I think it will be Golgotha.

Eugene B. Redmond, *Drumvoices: The Mission of Afro-American Poetry* (Garden City, NY: Anchor Press, 1976), pp. 198–200

NICHOLAS CANADAY   Although Arna Bontemps was taken by his parents to live in California in 1905 when he was three years old, he always maintained close emotional ties with his native state of Louisiana and with the South. Bontemps was born in Alexandria, Louisiana, in 1902, and his conscious memory of that town consisted mainly of some impressions about the backyard of a house at the corner of Ninth and Winn Streets and the sensation of being driven in a buggy across the bridge to Pineville on the other side of the Red River. His parents and grandparents were relatively comfortable Creoles, his father working in building construction, skilled as a brick and stone mason. Bontemps' father was, moreover, an accomplished musician, who blew his trombone in a band when time away from work was available. One of his father's older brothers lived in New Orleans, and that brother's daughter had married a prominent jazz player of the city by the name of Kid Ory.

Bontemps later learned about the sudden departure of his family from Louisiana. Returning home on a Saturday night after being paid his weekly wages, Bontemps' father encountered two white men who had just stepped out of a saloon and were blocking the sidewalk.

"Let's walk over the big nigger," one of them had said. The elder Bontemps had calmly stepped into the street and passed them by. But walking home that night, he had made the decision to move to California with his wife and two children. ⟨. . .⟩

Arna Bontemps thought of himself as a poet first, despite the fact that he was regarded in the Thirties as a novelist. His decision to move to Harlem in August of 1924 was partly motivated, he said years later, by his reading of Claude McKay's book of poetry, called *Harlem Shadows*. Published in 1922, McKay's book was enthusiastically received by young black intellectuals and aspiring writers. Arna Bontemps recalled putting his name on a waiting list to borrow the book from a Los Angeles public library. During the Twenties Bontemps published poems in various periodicals, his first published poem having appeared in the NAACP journal *Crisis* in 1924 before he left California. That bit of good fortune also quite naturally contributed to his desire to move to Harlem. The magazine *Crisis*, edited by W. E. B. Du Bois, gave an annual award beginning in 1921 for the best poem by a black writer printed in that journal. Bontemps' poem "Nocturne at Bethesda"—perhaps his best poem, certainly the one most anthologized—won the award in 1927. Earlier winners had included Langston Hughes and Jean Toomer. Bontemps also became a close friend of Countee Cullen, whose book of poems entitled *Color* (1925) Bontemps always considered the most important work of the early period of the Harlem Renaissance. Bontemps was best man in Cullen's 1928 marriage to Nina Yolande Du Bois—which marriage, however, ended in divorce. Bontemps later recalled, with a touch of wry irony, that he was also best man in Countee Cullen's second marriage in 1940 to Ida Mae Roberson.

Nicholas Canaday, "Arna Bontemps: The Louisiana Heritage," *Callaloo* 4, Nos. 1–3 (February–October 1981): 163–64

◈ *Bibliography*

God Sends Sunday. 1931.

Popo and Fifina, Children of Haiti (with Langston Hughes). 1932.

You Can't Pet a Possum. 1934.

Black Thunder: Gabriel's Revolt: Virginia: 1800. 1936.

Sad-Faced Boy. 1937.

Drums at Dusk. 1939.

Golden Slippers: An Anthology of Negro Poetry for Young Readers (editor). 1941.

Father of the Blues: An Autobiography by W. C. Handy (editor). 1941.

The Fast Sooner Hound (with Jack Conroy). 1942.

We Have Tomorrow. 1945.

They Seek a City (with Jack Conroy). 1945, 1966 (as *Anyplace But Here*).

Slappy Hooper, the Wonderful Sign Painter (with Jack Conroy). 1946.

American Missionary Association Archives in Fisk University. 1947.

Story of the Negro. 1948.

The Poetry of the Negro 1746–1949 (editor; with Langston Hughes). 1949, 1970.

George Washington Carver. 1950.

Sam Patch, the High, Wide, and Handsome Jumper (with Jack Conroy). 1951.

Chariot in the Sky: A Story of the Jubilee Singers. 1951.

The Story of George Washington Carver. 1954.

A List of Manuscripts, Published Works and Related Items in the Charles Waddell Chesnutt Collection of the Erastus Milo Cravath Memorial Library, Fisk University. 1954.

Lonesome Boy. 1955.

The Book of Negro Folklore (editor; with Langston Hughes). 1958.

Frederick Douglass: Slave, Fighter, Freeman. 1959.

100 Years of Negro Freedom. 1961.

American Negro Poetry (editor). 1963, 1974.

Personals. 1963.

I Too Sing America (with Langston Hughes). 1964.

Famous Negro Athletes. 1964.

Negro American Heritage (editor). 1968.

Great Slave Narratives (editor). 1969.

Hold Fast to Dreams: Poems Old and New (editor). 1969.

Mr. Kelso's Lion. 1970.

Free at Last: The Life of Frederick Douglass. 1971.

Young Booker: Booker T. Washington's Early Days. 1972.

The Harlem Renaissance Remembered (editor). 1972.

The Old South: "A Summer Tragedy" and Other Stories of the Thirties. 1973.

Arna Bontemps–Langston Hughes Letters 1925–1967. Ed. Charles H. Nichols. 1980.

Sterling A. Brown
1901–1989

STERLING ALLEN BROWN was born in Washington, D.C., on May 1, 1901. The last of six children, he was the son of a former slave, the Reverend Sterling Nelson Brown, the pastor of the Lincoln Temple Congregational Church and a professor of religion at Howard University. Stanley's mother, Adelaide Allen, was valedictorian at Fisk University and one of the original Jubilee Singers of Fisk, who introduced many spirituals to the general public.

Brown was raised in an atmosphere of literature and poetry, where bookshelves held such works as W. E. B. Du Bois's *The Souls of Black Folk,* the works of Alain Locke, and the histories of black life by Carter C. Woodson and Archibald H. Grimke.

In racially segregated Washington, D.C., Brown attended Lucretia Mott School, named after a well-known abolitionist and feminist. In Dunbar High School (named after the black writer Paul Laurence Dunbar), the young Sterling was a pupil of Haley Douglass, the grandson of Frederick Douglass, and of Neville Thomas, then president of the NAACP branch chapter. At this time, public schools were important in nurturing black pride; they were a source of great inner strength to many students and enabled Brown to enter Williams College, in Williamstown, Massachusetts.

At that time Williams, a small, exclusive liberal arts college, admitted only a handful of black students, and they were kept apart from the white students by school officials. Brown and his friends literally hid when playing jazz, then considered inappropriate listening matter for a member of the student body. However, Brown was most influenced by a literature professor, George Dutton, who introduced him to European literature. Brown was encouraged to read Flaubert, Henry James, and the novels of Sinclair Lewis, and he embraced critical realism, an approach in literature that was in vogue at that time. Modern American poetry, taught by Lewis Untermeyer, was also an influence on Brown, who upon graduation from Williams began to write poetry. The regionalism of Edwin Arlington Robinson, Robert Frost, Carl Sandburg, and A. E. Housman influenced the young poet.

16

Brown entered Harvard in 1922. Upon graduation, he immediately pursued his desire to teach and was employed as an English professor at Virginia Seminary in Lynchburg, Virginia, for three years. He subsequently taught at Lincoln University in Missouri (1926–28) and at Fisk University (1928–29). In 1929 he began what would be a forty-year teaching career at Howard University. Retiring in 1969, he resumed teaching in 1973 at the Howard University Institute for the Arts and Humanities, remaining there for two years.

Brown called himself an "amateur folklorist." He became interested in black culture and visited many black establishments in Nashville and other rural communities of the South. He loved the "yarnspinning" or oral tales told by such people as "Slam" in the Jefferson City Hotel and Calvin "Big Boy" Davis. Some of these tales find their way into his poetry.

Although Brown is best known as a poet—his first poetry volume was *Southern Road* (1932)—he wrote and edited several landmark works on black American fiction, poetry, and folklore. He was appointed the Federal Writers' Project's national editor for Negro affairs, serving from 1936 to 1940. His most important prose works were written at this time: *The Negro in American Fiction* and *Negro Poetry and Drama* (both 1937). With Arthur P. Davis and Ulysses Lee, he edited *The Negro Caravan* in 1941.

It is not clear why Brown published so little from 1941 to 1975. A book of poems, *No Hiding Place*, was rejected in 1937, leaving Brown embittered. The resurgence of interest in black literature in the 1960s and 1970s finally encouraged Brown—then regarded as a "living legend"—to issue *The Last Ride of Wild Bill and Eleven Narrative Poems* in 1975. Michael S. Harper edited Brown's *Collected Poems* in 1980. Sterling Brown died in Washington, D.C., on January 17, 1989.

▦ *Critical Extracts*

WILLIAM ROSE BENÉT   Sterling Brown (*Southern Road*) is a new negro poet to whom James Weldon Johnson introduces us in his foreword to Brown's book. Brown is of the "Younger Group" of negro writers. I myself think his work has distinctly more originality and power than that of Countee Cullen, and more range than that of Langston Hughes. Says Johnson:

> For his raw material he dug down into the deep mine of Negro folk poetry. He found the unfailing sources from which sprang the Negro folk epics and ballads such as "Stagolee," "John Henry," "Casey Jones," "Long Gone John," and others.

The fact that Brown is so good a narrative poet has inclined me toward him because of my particular interest in narrative verse. When he handles dialect he does so with precision and great effectiveness. A prime example of this is the colloquy between "Old Man Buzzard" and young Fred. Brown can also command real pathos and grimness. His Sam Smiley, the buck dancer, was taught by the whites in the Great War to rip up bellies with a bayonet. When he came back from the war and found that a rich white man had ruined his girl, he retaliated by killing him. But the poem ends in no breakdown into sentimentality. ⟨. . .⟩

Of the younger negro poets, I consider Sterling A. Brown to be the most versatile and the least derivative.

William Rose Benét, "A New Negro Poet," *Saturday Review of Literature,* 14 May 1932, p. 732

STERLING BROWN   *Southern Road* by Sterling A. Brown (1932) is chiefly an attempt at folk portraiture of southern characters. Brown sought to convey the tragedy of the southern Negro, in poems like the title poem, "Children of The Mississippi," "King of Cotton" and "Sam Smiley," and the comedy in the Slim Greer series and "Sporting Beasley." The wandering roustabout is recorded in "Long Gone" and "Odyssey of Big Boy." The irony to be found in Negro folk-song appears in "Mr. Samuel and Sam." "Strong Man," making use of a refrain found in Sandburg—"The strong men keep coming on"—is an expression of the dogged stoicism Brown has found in Negro experience. He has made a fairly close study of folk-ways and folk-songs, and has used this in interpreting folk-experience and character which he considers one of the important tasks of Negro poetry. He is not afraid of using folk-speech, refusing to believe dialect to be "an instrument of only two stops—pathos and humor." He uses free verse and the traditional forms as well as folk-forms, and many of his poems are subjective. His second volume, to be called *No Hiding Place*, re-explores the southern scene with more emphasis on social themes.

Sterling Brown, *Negro Poetry and Drama* (Washington, DC: Associates in Negro Folk Education, 1937), pp. 76–77

DAVID LITTLEJOHN   Brown, a professor at Howard University, made a vigorous and intelligent attempt to do for the Southern Negro what Langston Hughes had done for the Northern, in a series of ballad-like narrative tales of racial protest: chants, chain-gang songs, stories, and the like. His irony was sharp, his ideas were exciting; he was one of the first protestors-in-verse (and there were many) to pay heed to the basic demands of good poetry. Some of his poems, with their hammer-driving freedoms, their guitar-picking rhythms, have the poignant authenticity of folk song. He lacked, unfortunately, any real organic verbal skill, so his poetry still resided more in his ideas, in the affects of underplayed indirection, than in the total achievement. But it was right for the time, and it remains a strong indictment.

David Littlejohn, *Black on White: A Critical Survey of Writing by American Negroes* (New York: Grossman Publishers, 1966), p. 62

ARTHUR P. DAVIS   The poetry of Sterling Brown deals mainly with the following general subjects: the *endurance* of the Negro, the stark tragedy which is too often his lot, death as a means of release from his misery, the open road as another escape, and humor as a safety valve. Most of his work may be classed as protest poetry in the classical sense of that now frowned-on term. Brown has been influenced by Negro folk material, by such poets as Sandburg and Frost, and, of course, by the corpus of English and American traditional poetry. His poetical forms reflect all of these influences.

He uses the sonnet form (though not too often), stanzaic forms, the free-verse patterns of the New Poets, and ballad and blues forms, the last-named both in the conventional pattern and in patterns derived from the conventional form. His language is simple, suggestive, and direct, reflecting strongly his interest in the speech of the folk. Several of his best poems use contrapuntally statements in standard English with statements from the reservoir of folk comment (usually given in italics). There is a quality in Brown's poetry that makes it quite different from that of Langston Hughes, although both tended to use the same folk subjects and forms. Brown has more intensity and a deeper concern for dramatic effect. This is not a value judgment concerning the quality of the works of the two poets; it is merely a comparison of the impressions made on one reader. ⟨. . .⟩

In the face of such overwhelming odds, what keeps the black man going, what makes him stubbornly *endure?* Three things, Professor Brown seems to suggest in answer to that question: the Negro's religion, his song, and his ability to laugh not only at "Cap'n Charlie" but also at himself. Taking religion first—Sister Lou could not have made it without a deep and comforting sense of a world to come. The speaker and adviser in "Sister Lou" gives her friend specific and reassuring instructions: "Honey / Don't be feared of them pearly gates, / Don't go 'round to de back, / No mo, dataway / Not evah no mo'." In the homey speech of Southern Christian folk, the poet paints a heaven of release, not only from having to go to the back doors, but also a heaven in which Sister Lou can assume a simple dignity no poor black woman can find in this world. It is a place where she, for once, can be *somebody*. This thought has been a rock weary land for countless oppressed blacks.

The Negro's song, whether spirituals or blues, has been a safety valve. A singer like Ma Rainey expressed the sorrow and the misery of the lives of poor black folks, and her singing brings release through catharsis:

> O Ma Rainey,
> Li'l an' low
> Sing us 'bout de hard luck
> Roun' our do';
> Sing us 'bout de lonesome road
> We mus' go. . . .

The Negro's ability to laugh, to keep from crying, has helped to keep his sanity in a world that has been irrationally against him. After reading the bitter poems of Sterling Brown, one is surprised to find that he also has a rich sense of humor. Poems like "Mister Samuel and Sam," "Checkers," "Scotty Has His Say," and the Slim Greer series show not only Brown's ability to laugh and to protest but also his deep knowledge of the life of ordinary black people and the ways of white folks. To his comment on the human weakness of black and white, the poet adds a special ingredient from folk humor: the tall tale. In "Slim Greer," "Slim Lands a Job," "Slim in Atlanta," and "Slim in Hell," Brown has created not only a new American folk character, but has elevated the tall story into a sophisticated art.

Arthur P. Davis, *From the Dark Tower: Afro-American Writers 1900 to 1960* (Washington, DC: Howard University Press, 1974), pp. 127, 129–30

BLYDEN JACKSON   Born and brought up in Washington, D.C., and educated in two schools of the Ivy League, Brown was unquestionably a member in good standing of the Talented Tenth, at least in terms of his upbringing and his personal attainments. Insofar, however, as his art was concerned, whether in terms of his practice or his profession, he was a New Negro, and a New Negro, indeed, of a very genuine kind. He had steeped himself in the lore and legends that circulated among the Negro folk. He had listened to Negro speech, the commonest and most ordinary Negro speech, and listened well. He had observed, and perceived in their significance, the jobs which Negroes without "status" were permitted to perform. He had done likewise with the conduct of such Negroes in their private, separate world when they were free from the constrictions which they placed upon themselves when they thought that the wrong people might be keeping an eye on them. His Big Boy in the "Odyssey of Big Boy" drives steel, strips tobacco, mines coal, shucks corn, cultures rice, works docks, waits tables, and washes dishes as he ambles through a subculture from Louisiana to New England. As Brown's Big Boy roves and works, moreover, he disports himself in the arms of women endowed with a wide variety of charms, and colors— with a "stovepipe blond" (that is, a very black girl) in Macon, a yellow girl in Maryland, a chocolate brown in Richmond, and a Creole woman of easy virtue in New Orleans, not to mention the best girl of them all, a Washingtonian (color not mentioned) at "Four'n half and M." Big Boy, that is, belongs to the breed of John Henry and Stagolee.

In Brown's poetry Big Boy is not alone. In "When De Saints Go Ma'ching Home" a Negro gleeman of Big Boy's breed, armed with a guitar, after regaling an audience with "bawdy songs and blues," surrenders once more, as he always seems to do in his finale to an evening's repertoire, to a penchant for brooding over his own past. The guitarist chants a requiem of sorts for the "saints"—people he has known in a life as much that of a rover as Big Boy's—most of them black, who (unlike the sinners of his acquaintance, about some of whom he also croons) will have welcome access to the land beyond the Jordan. In "Frankie and Johnny" Brown takes into his own hands the well-known American ballad and reshapes it into an acid disquisition on that, for three hundred years, especially sensitive area of American personal behavior, the relationship between black men and white women. Thus he sets his poem in the South, converting his Frankie into a half-witted poor-white girl with a sadistic streak in her demented outlook on the world and his Johnny into an earnest young Negro whom she tantalizes with her body until he can no longer restrain himself from physical intimacies with her (consummated, with great aptness for allegory, between the rows of cotton) that lead to Johnny's lynching.

Blyden Jackson, "From One 'New Negro' to Another," *Black Poetry in America: Two Essays in Historical Interpretation* by Blyden Jackson and Louis D. Rubin, Jr. (Baton Rouge: Louisiana State University Press, 1974), pp. 58–60

CHARLES H. ROWELL   "What motivates a middle-class Black man and a Harvard graduate . . . to devote his life to portraying less well-to-do folks?" queries Genevieve Ekaete. She answers:

> Being Black is the key. . . . According to [Sterling Brown], he was indignant at the corrupted folk speech publicized by "white comic writers like Octavus Roy Cohen." From his experience, Brown says, he knew his people didn't talk that way. It wasn't enough for him to enjoin them to "Stop knowing it all!" He had to bring some semblance of balance by putting his people down on black and white to counter the proliferating distortions from other sources. ⟨"Sterling Brown: A Living Legend," *New Directions*, Winter 1974.⟩

Then, too, early in his teaching career Brown "read the new realistic poetry in American life"—that of Frost, Sandburg, Masters, Lindsay and Robinson, for example. In their "democratic approach to the people," Brown saw much that reflected his own thoughts about ordinary people. Brown recalls: "when Carl Sandburg said 'yes' to the American people, I wanted to say 'yes' to my people." Brown's "yes" was to give us carefully wrought poems portraying "common" black folk "in a manner constant with them." His "yes" to black people was also to give us a series of critical works which attempted to counter "the proliferating distortions" of black folk life and character. As early as the Twenties, Brown began writing a series of critical studies and reviews on the portrayal of blacks in American literature. In 1929, he observed that

> From Kennedy's "Swallow Barn," about the first treatment of the plantation, down to Dixon's rabid Ku Klux Klan propaganda, the Negro has been shown largely as an animal. Kennedy, doing a piece of special pleading, showed the Negro as parasitical, excessively loyal, contented, irresponsible, and so forth. Dixon showed his Negro characters, not as faithful dogs, but as mad curs. His brutes are given to rapine, treachery, bestiality, and gluttony.

Like other New Negro writers, Brown knew that such portrayals were neither accurate characterizations nor true expressions of the souls of black folk.

After study at Williams and Harvard, Brown prepared himself to counter distorting images of black people perpetuated in American literature. To do so, he read widely and critically into the literature by and about black people, and carefully studied Afro-American history and folk culture. Hence his *Negro Poetry and Drama, The Negro in American Fiction* (both 1937), and several important periodical essays and reviews—sources which no serious student of American literature can ignore. But to counter the distorting images as poet, Brown knew that he had to go beyond books and his Washington experiences for material: he went directly to black people in the South. That is, as he taught and traveled in the South, he lived among and carefully observed those peasants who created black folk traditions—traditions which sustained them in their daily lives. Writing in 1934 about Brown as "folk poet," Alain Locke asserted that

> Sterling Brown has listened long and carefully to the folk in their intimate hours, when they are talking to themselves, not, so to speak, as in Dunbar, but actually as they do when the masks of protective mimicry fall. Not only has he dared to give quiet but bold expression to this private thought and speech, but he has dared to give the Negro peasant credit for thinking.

In a word, when Brown taught and traveled in the South, he became an insider to the multifarious traditions and verbal art forms indigenous to black folk, and through his adaptations of their verbal art forms and spirit he, as poet, became an instrument for their myriad voices. Hence *Southern Road*.

Charles H. Rowell, "Sterling A. Brown and the Afro-American Folk Tradition," *Studies in the Literary Imagination* 7, No. 2 (Fall 1974): 133–34

STERLING STUCKEY   In ways both subtle and obvious Sterling Nelson Brown, distinguished minister and father of the poet, influenced his son's attitude toward life and literature. Born a slave in eastern Tennessee, the elder Brown, unlike many of similar origin, was not ashamed of his slave heritage, nor was he ashamed of rural Negro descendants of slaves. The sense of continuity with the past and the considerable attention devoted to the folk Negro in Brown's poetry probably owe as much to his having been the son of such a father as they do to the valuable experiences which the young poet had in the South following his graduation from Williams College and Harvard University.

Fortunately Sterling A. Brown, exposed to the critical realist approach to literature of George Dutton of Williams and the realism that characterized some of the best of American poetry of the twenties, especially the work of Edwin Arlington Robinson, Robert Frost, and Carl Sandburg, was all the more prepared to take an uncondescending, that is to say genuinely respectful, attitude toward the folk whom he encountered in the South. And there he discovered a wealth of folk material waiting to be fashioned into art, and a number of quite ordinary people who, thanks to his artistry, would teach us unusual things about life. Brown realized the need to explore the life of the Southern Negro below the surface in order to reveal unseen aspects of his being, his strength and fortitude, his healing humor, and his way of confronting tragedy. As a young man he began meeting and talking to a variety of people, some of whom, such as Big Boy Davis, a traveling guitar player after whom the character in "Southern Road," the title poem, is modeled, would win permanent places in our literature. The fact that Brown, with his sharp eye, fine ear, and excellent mind, spent so many of his early years in the South helps us understand the sensibility behind a volume which reads like the work of a gifted poet who has lived a lifetime.

Just as Brown's creation of folk characters presents individualized portraits revelatory of interior lives, his uses of the great body of Negro music, of the Spirituals, Blues, Jazz, and Work Songs, extend rather than reflect meanings. Sadly enough, there is reason to believe that many students of Negro literature ⟨. . .⟩ are unfamiliar with most of the poems in *Southern Road*. Numerous major poems have never been anthologized; and some, such as "Cabaret," have only recently been brought to our attention by critics. Yet a specialist on the "Harlem Renaissance," of which Brown was not a part, *places him in that movement* with a number of references, including one to "Memphis Blues," while omitting mention of "Cabaret," perhaps the single most important New Negro Movement poem dealing with the exploitation of Negro performing artists, especially members of orchestras and chorus lines, during the twenties and since.

Though "Cabaret" is by no means the only significant Brown poem that numerous scholars don't seem to know exists, it deserves attention because of its brilliant multi-level interplay between appearance and reality: between life as Negroes live it and life as projected onto them by white audiences. "Cabaret" stands as a starkly eloquent emblem of the frustrations, cleverly masked, of Negro entertainers before the bizarre expectations of white patrons of black arts of the twenties. The inexorably grim logic of the poem unfolds to the accompaniment of Negro music in a Chicago Black and Tan club in 1927. The poet employs symbolically the Blues, Jazz, the corruptions of Tin Pan Alley, the perversions of genuine Negro music, the dirty misuse of Negro chorus girls and musicians—all set against the rural tragedy of a desperate people in the terrible flood of 1927.

> Sterling Stuckey, "Introduction" (1974), *The Collected Poems of Sterling A. Brown*, ed. Michael S. Harper (New York: Harper & Row, 1980), pp. 9–10

MICHAEL S. HARPER   His poems are *made*, born of vision and revision, as a sculptor chisels, and Brown does, or a painter paints; biography is not poetry, but poetry demands a life fully lived—the poem is the performance. Sterling Brown's sense of design, of composition as a rigorous discipline, instructs and informs and extends a continuous consciousness of history and literary form. His own heroic ideal—*been down so long that down don't worry me*—is an abiding commitment to the word made flesh. His poetry teaches in the sense that it illustrates a clarity and precision of form as the skeletal structure of the expressive designs of language, and that language has a purity of diction because the poet's selectivity is the voice of authority—he controls the atmosphere, cadence, and pace of utterance,

activating the landscape and voicings of the poem, while disarming his
reader, his hearer. Brown's poems are deceptively literate; they move as
images created and controlled as activation, as an agency of contract; in
this sense he is a great poet of community. Brown's world is grounded in
his perceptual faith in the long haul, and in the spirit which needs no
hiding.

> Michael S. Harper, "Preface," *The Collected Poems of Sterling A. Brown* (New York:
> Harper & Row, 1980), p. xiii

JOANNE V. GABBIN   One of the New Negro writers to emerge
during the early 1930s, Sterling A. Brown attempted to represent Black life
against the aesthetic background of the Black folk and cultural tradition.
He, along with such writers as Jean Toomer, James Weldon Johnson, and
Langston Hughes, explored folk art as a way of understanding and interpreting the truth concerning the life and character of Black Americans. Brown,
using the folk tradition as a prism through which to see the Black experience,
also infused his own poetry with folk themes, symbols, forms, and narrative
techniques in an effort to express more fully the ethos of Black life. A survey
of his poetry will reveal an extensive absorption of the folk tradition, as
well as the complex sensibility of a self-conscious artist who has a firm
grounding in the American critical realism and other literary traditions.

In fact, Brown's skill as a poet is clearly demonstrated in his ability to
synthesize the diverse traditions at hand. This process of synthesis Brown
prefers to call "cross-pollination" and credits it with the creation of some
of his best poetry. For example, in the comic ballad "Slim in Hell," Brown
crosses the ancient legend of Orpheus and Eurydice with the elaborate lore
of the folk trickster and presents them in the socio-historical context of
twentieth-century Dixie. The result is a vigorous product that maintains
the strength of both traditions, while simultaneously exhibiting vital new
combinations and varieties.

As Brown explores the fertile field of oral literary traditions, the folk
tradition shows the greatest vitality and, consequently, has a strong influence
on his poetry. However, the impress of the American tradition of critical
realism in shaping, sharpening, and deepening his treatment of folk material
is also significant. Brown joins the democratic voices of Robinson, Frost,
and Sandburg as they say "yes" to their people. Often in a voice that melds

the American vernacular with the folk speech, Brown says a resounding "yes" as he has his compelling portraits and narratives reveal the reality and vision of America. ⟨. . .⟩

With the publication of his first volume of poetry in 1932, Sterling A. Brown introduced what was to be his most pervasive metaphor, the Southern Road. As one scholar of Brown's poetry writes, Brown "adopted one of the most persistent symbols and thematic motifs in folklore to unify *Southern Road.*"

> The road has been a central metaphor in the black experience, and it has been essential that the traveler keep "movering," "keep inchin' along." As a symbol, the road takes various forms: the river, the railroad, the Underground Railroad, the road to Glory, the road to Freedom, the way of survival, the path winding through the lonesome valley, the hard road of Life. It could not have been by accident that Brown selected the road as his central symbol, entitled his book *Southern Road,* and derived his themes from the implications of that symbol. ⟨Betty S. Barber⟩

In the initial quotation on the frontispiece of the book, the road is transformed into a path of knowledge and experience.

> O de ole sheep dey knows de road,
> Young lambs gotta find de way. (Spiritual)

By extension, the road becomes the road of life itself, the path from childhood to old age, from naiveté to wisdom. Appropriately, these lines suggest Brown's purpose in *Southern Road* and in several poems that followed its publication. Once taught by wise "ole sheep" the ways of the folk, he intends to construct a road that will link the cultural past with the New Negro awareness, establishing, as Alain Locke claimed, "a sort of common denominator between the old and new Negro" and giving credence to the idea that the Black literary tradition is one continuous line of development issuing from the earliest folk thought and utterance.

Joanne V. Gabbin, *Sterling A. Brown: Building the Black Aesthetic Tradition* (Westport, CT: Greenwood Press, 1985), pp. 117–19

ROBERT B. STEPTO   Brown *wrote* himself into the Renaissance, in his contribution to blues poetry and in his two major sequences of what

I am persuaded to call Renaissance poetry. In the field of blues poetry, Brown matched Langston Hughes step by step, or, innovation by innovation, when he duplicated classic blues forms in poems such as "Tin Roof Blues," and when he successfully simulated entire, communally contextualized blues performances in poems including "Ma Rainey." Where he went beyond Hughes was in his singular creations of blues quatrains. ⟨. . .⟩

Brown was inside the Renaissance in that he, like Hughes, declared, "I, too, sing America," and outside in that, unlike Hughes, he really meant what he said. How he went his own way is best seen in the fact that this art was far more affected by the flood of 1927 than by cabaret life or Marcus Garvey (though he wrote of cabarets and Garvey, too). In this regard, he was more like Ma Rainey and Bessie Smith than like the average Renaissance writer, and that probably was to his benefit.

The Renaissance gains in stature when our definitions of it allow a place for Sterling Brown, and if our definitions do not offer him a place then they need to be changed. Brown's blues poems are superior to Hughes's; his *Southern Road* rivals Toomer's *Cane* as a presentation of Negro American geography; his portraits of the folk, rural and urban, and his renderings of their speech, have no match.

> Robert B. Stepto, "Sterling A. Brown: Outsider in the Harlem Renaissance?," *The Harlem Renaissance: Revaluations*, ed. Amrajit Singh, William S. Shiver, and Stanley Brodwin (New York: Garland, 1989), pp. 77–80

CHARLES H. ROWELL and STERLING BROWN   ROW-
ELL: In his preface to the 1968 combined edition of your *Negro Poetry and Drama* and *The Negro in American Fiction*, Robert Bone describes your studies as "comprehensive surveys in the field of iconography, tracing through American fiction, poetry, and drama the changing image of the Negro. Their real focus," he says, "is a sociology of literature, the politics of culture. They are concerned with the uses and abuses of the image-making function in society." It seems to me that your studies are more than a sociology of literature.

BROWN: I think Bone is straining there to stay in with the New Critics. It was an ungenerous introduction. He speaks, for instance, of its not being great criticism, but who in the world is writing great criticism today? You keep the phrase "great criticism" for Matthew Arnold. . . . Bone knew that the book was written for a very definite purpose, and he knew that the book had to be confined. You see, I could not write at full in the book. This was part of a series and it had to be a certain length and so I was kept down. But I have just as much literary criticism of many of those novels as he did in his work that was devoted only to Negro novelists. He worked under me. I was his advisor on his thesis, you see. He knew that. I never meant the book as great criticism. I stated what the book was. I had two jobs to do: I had to evaluate the books, and I also had to discuss certain stereotypes. I think I did in the book as a whole. I think I did it better in *The Negro in American Fiction* than in *Negro Poetry and Drama*, because the confined space was just too much to handle poetry and drama. I got in trouble with Alain Locke who edited the series because I ran *The Negro in American Fiction* a little longer than I was supposed to; I was to keep it to 125 pages, but I just couldn't do it. A lot of stuff I wanted to say I . . . but my criticism of single works is running through *Opportunity,* a magazine. . . . Anybody who ever took a course from me knows that I always paid attention to the craft of fiction. I pay attention to craft, but in this book there was a whole lot to do, to cover the range of American fiction with all of its stupidity and all of its ignorance and to prove it. Most people just dismiss books and say that the white man is stereotyping. Of course, I didn't do that. Most of the white books were stereotyping blacks, but some were not. ⟨. . .⟩

ROWELL: I think Zora Neale Hurston ⟨. . .⟩ accused Locke of not having a real knowledge of black folk tradition. She said he sat and listened to what other people said and then wrote about the tradition.

BROWN: That is not fair. She was angry. She fell out with most men. She was an early women's liberator. She was kicked around. She had much right on her side. She fought with Langston Hughes. She fought with Dick Wright, and she wrote a bad attack on Dick Wright. She fought with me, because of what I said about her novel called *Their Eyes Were Watching God*, which I think is a good novel. It is the best thing she ever did. *Mules and Men* is second. On that novel I stressed the hard lives the people on the farm lived. I stressed this from a viewpoint of social realism. She said I wasn't going to make a communist out of her, and she turned away. But now, see, she was all involved with Fannie Hurst with whom I had a big quarrel. Zora Neale [Hurston] was involved with literary patrons in New York City. I never had any dealings with those people. I don't even know what's in the Van Vechten business at Yale because of my distaste for the man. I have tremendous distaste for Carl Van Vechten. I don't ever say "Harlem Renaissance," because it wasn't Harlem. It was the "Negro Renaissance." What I disliked was black writers' reliance on Van Vechten and their acceptance of his leadership. I felt that he set up an exotic primitive. His heart was not really with us in that he was a voyeur. I'm doing an essay in this book for the Howard University Press called "Carl Van Vechten Voyeur and Robert Penn Warren Informer." Both of them are very false friends. Zora Neale was very friendly to us. She came here, sat on the sofa there [pointing] and told us some stories. She was a beautiful storyteller; she was a wonderful actress. She knew a lot of stuff, and I think she's been underestimated. She battled, and she battled men. She had some grouch. I didn't know this little thing you told me about Locke. ⟨. . .⟩ She couldn't get along with people.

> Charles H. Rowell and Sterling A. Brown, " 'Let Me Be with Ole Jazzbo': An Interview with Sterling A. Brown," *Callaloo* 14, No. 4 (Fall 1991): 803–5

⊞ *Bibliography*

Outline for the Study of the Poetry of American Negroes. 1931.

Southern Road. 1932.

The Negro in American Fiction. 1937.

Negro Poetry and Drama. 1937.

The Negro Caravan: Writings by American Negroes (editor; with Arthur P. Davis and Ulysses Lee). 1941.

The Last Ride of Wild Bill and Eleven Narrative Poems. 1975.

Collected Poems. Ed. Michael S. Harper. 1980.

Countee Cullen
1903–1946

COUNTEE CULLEN was born Countee Leroy Porter on May 30, 1903. Although both New York City and Baltimore have been cited as his birthplace, he was probably born in Louisville, Kentucky. Orphaned in childhood, he was raised by a Mrs. Porter, who was probably his grandmother. In his teens he was adopted by African Methodist Episcopal Church minister Frederick Asbury Cullen and his wife, Carolyn, who encouraged Countee to write. Cullen's poetry was already seeing regular publication by the time he graduated from New York University in 1925. His first book, *Color*, appeared that same year; Cullen won the Harmon Gold Award and critical praise for his Keatsian verse and his frank depiction of racial prejudice.

Cullen received an M.A. from Harvard in 1926, then became assistant editor of the National Urban League journal *Opportunity*. In 1927 he published the acclaimed *Copper Sun* and *The Ballad of the Brown Girl*, and edited *Caroling Dusk*, an historic anthology of work by black poets. The following year he married Yolande Du Bois, daughter of W. E. B. Du Bois, and traveled to Paris on a Guggenheim Fellowship. Yolande filed for divorce before he returned; their relationship inspired the tortured love poetry of *The Black Christ and Other Poems* (1929).

Back in the United States, Cullen published a novel of life in Harlem, *One Way to Heaven* (1932), and a verse adaptation of Euripides' *Medea* (1935). From 1932 to 1945 Cullen settled into a teaching position at a junior high school in New York City. In 1940 he married Ida Mae Roberson and published a children's book of verse entitled *The Lost Zoo (A Rhyme for the Young, but Not Too Young)*, sharing the bylines with his pet, Christopher Cat. Two years later he published a prose work for children, *My Lives and How I Lost Them*, which purported to be Christopher's autobiography. Cullen authored and coauthored a number of plays, most of which were not published; his own selection of his best poems was published posthumously as *On These I Stand: An Anthology of the Best Poems of Countee Cullen* (1947).

Countee Cullen died on January 9, 1946. Gerald Early has now assembled Cullen's collected writings under the title *My Soul's High Song* (1991).

◈ *Critical Extracts*

CARL VAN VECHTEN   What the colored race needs to break its bonds is a few more men and women of genius. This is a theory recently promulgated by the Negro intelligentsia. Providence, apparently, is willing to test the theory, for genius, or talent, is pouring prodigally out of Harlem, and out of other cities' Black Belts as well. Such young writers as Jean Toomer, Jessie Fauset, Walter White, Claude McKay, Eric Walrond, Langston Hughes, Rudolph Fisher, and Alain Locke; such young musicians, actors, and dancers as Roland Hayes, Paul Robeson, Julius Bledsoe, Laurence Brown, Eddie Rector, Florence Mills, and Johnny Hudgins (I am naming only a few of the many) are sufficient earnest of what the "gift of black folk" (to employ Dr. Du Bois's poetic phrase) will be in the immediate future.

One of the best of the Negro writers, Countee Cullen, is the youngest of them all. He was barely twenty-one when "The Shroud of Color" (published in the November 1924 issue of the *American Mercury*) created a sensation analogous to that created by the appearance of Edna St. Vincent Millay's "Renascence" in 1912, lifting its author at once to a position in the front rank of contemporary American poets, white or black. "The Shroud of Color" was emotional in its passionate eloquence, but Countee Cullen sometimes ⟨. . .⟩ strikes the strings of his inspirational lyre more lightly, although a satiric or bitter aftertaste is likely to linger in his most ostensibly flippant verse. All his poetry is characterized by a suave, unpretentious, brittle, intellectual elegance; some of it—"To John Keats, Poet, at Spring Time" is an excellent example—by a haunting, lyric loveliness. It is to be noted that, like any distinguished artist of any race, he is able to write stanzas which have no bearing on the problems of his own race. In this respect his only Negro forebear, so far as I can recall at the moment, is the poet Pushkin, whose verses dwelt on Russian history and folklore, although he was the great-grandson of a slave.

> Carl Van Vechten, "Countee Cullen: A Note by Carl Van Vechten," *Vanity Fair* 24, No. 4 (June 1925): 62

JESSIE FAUSET   *Color* is the name of Mr. Cullen's book and color is, rightly, in every sense its prevailing characteristic. For not only does every bright glancing line abound in color but it is also in another sense the yard-stick by which all the work in this volume is measured. Thus his poems fall into three categories: Those, and these are very few, in which no mention is made of color; those in which the adjectives "black" or "brown" or "ebony" are deliberately introduced to show that the type which the author had in mind was not white; and thirdly the poems which arise out of the conscious of being a "Negro in a day like this" in America.

These last are not only the most beautifully done but they are by far the most significant group in the book. I refer especially to poems of the type of "Yet Do I Marvel", "The Shroud of Color", "Heritage" and "Pagan Prayer". It is in such work as this that the peculiar and valuable contribution of the American colored man is to be made to American literature. For any genuine poet black or white might have written "Oh for a Little While Be Kind" or the lines to "John Keats"; the idea contained in a "Song of Praise" was used long ago by an old English poet and has since been set to music by Roger Quilter. But to pour forth poignantly and sincerely the feelings which make plain to the world the innerness of the life which black men live calls for special understanding. Cullen has packed into four illuminating lines the psychology of colored Americans, that strange extra dimension which totally artificial conditions have forced into sharp reality. He writes:

> All day long and all night through,
> One thing only must I do:
> Quench my pride and cool my blood,
> Lest I perish in the flood.

That is the new expression of the struggle now centuries old. Here I am convinced is Mr. Cullen's forte; he has the feeling and the gift to express colored-ness in a world of whiteness. I hope he will not be deflected from continuing to do that of which he has made such a brave and beautiful beginning. I hope that no one crying down "special treatment" will turn him from his native and valuable genre. There *is* no "universal treatment"; it is all specialized. When Kipling spoke of having the artist to

> paint the thing as he sees it
> For the God of things as they are,

he set the one infallible rule by which all workmanship should be conceived, achieved and judged. In a time when it is the vogue to make much of the

Negro's aptitude for clownishness or to depict him objectively as a serio-
comic figure, it is a fine and praiseworthy act for Mr. Cullen to show through
the interpretation of his own subjectivity the inner workings of the Negro
soul and mind.

Jessie Fauset, [Review of *Color*], *Crisis* 31, No. 5 (March 1926): 238–39

J. SAUNDERS REDDING   Now undoubtedly the biggest, single
unalterable circumstance in the life of Mr. Cullen is his color. Most of the
life he has lived has been influenced by it. And when he writes by it, he
writes; but when this does not guide him, his pen trails faded ink across his
pages.

To argue long about Countee Cullen—his ideas, his poetic creed, and
the results he obtains—is to come face to face with the poet's own confusion.
It is not a matter of words or language merely, as it was with Dunbar: it is
a matter of ideas and feelings. Once Mr. Cullen wrote: "Negro verse (as a
designation, that is) would be more confusing than accurate. Negro poetry,
it seems to me, in the sense that we speak of Russian, French, or Chinese
poetry, must emanate from some country other than this in some language
other than our own."

At another time: "Somehow or other I find my poetry of itself treating
of the Negro, of his joys and his sorrows—mostly of the latter—, and of
the heights and depths of emotion which I feel as a Negro."

And still another:

> Then call me traitor if you must,
> Shout treason and default!
> Saying I betray a sacred trust
> Aching beyond this vault.
> I'll bear your censure as your praise,
> For never shall the clan
> Confine my singing to its ways
> Beyond the ways of man.

The answer to all this seems to be: Chinese poetry translated into English
remains Chinese poetry—Chinese in feeling, in ideas.

But there is no confusion in Mr. Cullen's first volume, *Color*, which is
far and away his best. Here his poetry (nearly all of it on racial subjects, or
definitely and frankly conditioned by race) helps to balance the savage

poetic outbursts of Claude McKay. Countee Cullen is decidedly a gentle poet, a schoolroom poet whose vision of life is interestingly distorted by too much of the vicarious. This lends rather than detracts. It is as though he saw life through the eyes of a woman who is at once shrinking and bold, sweet and bitter. His province is the nuance, the finer shades of feeling, subtility and finesse of emotion and expression. Often however, with feline slyness, he bares the pointed talons of a coolly ironic and deliberate humor which is his way of expressing his resentment at the racial necessities.

J. Saunders Redding, *To Make a Poet Black* (Chapel Hill: University of North Carolina Press, 1939), pp. 109–10

BERTRAM L. WOODRUFF   The poet, ⟨. . .⟩ by using his creative power to change sadness into gladness, is able to offer consolation to men. With the healing force of its high ideals of Love, Beauty, Faith in Man, and Christian Belief, poetry is a balm for the evils and frustrations of life. Cullen tells of the confidence in the healing power of poetry possessed by the Irish poets whom he met at Padraic Colum's:

> I walked in a room where Irish poets were;
> I saw the muse enthroned, heard how they worshipped her,
> Felt men nor gods could never so envenon them
> That Poetry could pass and they not grasp her hem,
> Not cry on her for healing. ⟨"After a Visit"⟩

Inasmuch as Cullen confesses in the same poem that there had been a gulf between his aesthetic theory and his experience, there is no doubt of the intellectual and emotional dissension within his being concerning the meaning of life. As he himself acknowledges,

> There is a thorn forever in his breast,
> Who cannot take his world for what it seems.
>   ⟨"A Thorn Forever in the Breast"⟩

Cullen, as a Negro, cannot take life in America for what it seems to him. Writing once of the race conflict in America and the natural beauty of the South, he exclaimed, "If only the South loved the Negro as he is capable of loving her—there is no end to what might be." He yearns for an abiding place in America where, as in France, "fair and kindly" folk may offer "what was denied my hungry heart at home." But the tie with America is too "taut to be undone." Cullen has posed the question, "This ground and I are we not one?"

All in all, Cullen's philosophy is a tentative ordering of what is inchoate in his experience. If his poetic intuition fails to bring order out of chaos, it is not because he is a victim of self-deception. His poetry reveals his sincere attempt to discern whatever spiritual adjustment there may be for suffering, passionate, and weak souls in a hostile world. In the treatment of his poetic themes he sifts minutely the wheat from the chaff of human ideals, leaving as hoped-for verities his faith in Love, Beauty, Mankind, the Sacrifice of Christ, and Poetry. In his moments of weakness and doubt, he feels too keenly the everlasting strife and frustration in the world and the awesome mystery of Death.

The thorn forever in his breast has prevented Countee Cullen from maintaining in his poetry the spiritual serenity and strength that may be felt, at times, in the core of his writings. Instead of sentimentalizing the anguish created by the thorn, he would do well to resolve the problem by holding fast to his "Faith the canny conjuror." Some day, perhaps, he may write fully of his "own soul's ecstasy," since he has already written what might be adopted as a personal and poetic creed:

> I count it little being barred
> From those who undervalue me.
> I have my own soul's ecstasy.
> Men may not bind the summer sea,
> Nor set a limit to the stars;
> The sun seeps through all iron bars;
> The moon is ever manifest.
> These things my heart always possessed.
> And more than this (and here's the crown)
> No man, my son, can batter down
> The star-flung ramparts of the mind.
> ⟨The Black Christ⟩

Bertram L. Woodruff, "The Poetic Philosophy of Countee Cullen," *Phylon* 1, No. 3 (September 1940): 222–23

HARVEY CURTIS WEBSTER   Reading and rereading the selections Cullen himself made from his six volumes of verse, one re-experiences the varied reactions his career provoked. *Color* (1925) promised more than any other first volume that had been written by an American Negro.

Although most of the poems were about social-racial ironies, the range of substance was very broad compared, say, to the range of ⟨Paul Laurence⟩ Dunbar or ⟨James Weldon⟩ Johnson. He wrote compressedly and movingly of "A Brown Girl Dead," wittily of the lady he knew who

> thinks that up in heaven
> Her class lies late and snores,
> While poor black cherubs rise at seven
> To do celestial chores;

with restrained protestantism of the difficulties of being an American Negro ("Incident"; "Saturday's Child"; "Yet do I marvel at this curious thing: / To make a poet black, and bid him sing!"); with infectious gaiety of "She of the Dancing Feet":

> And what would I do in heaven, pray,
> Me with my dancing feet,
> And limbs like apple boughs that sway
> When the gusty rain winds beat?

He also wrote phonily of his presumptively uncivilized heart and head in such poems as "The Shroud of Color" and "Heritage" (unfortunately these two poems accorded best with most critics' view of Negro nature and were most praised), competently and uncompellingly on such subjects as the wise dead and "To John Keats, Poet, at Spring Time." Altogether, it seemed that Cullen was an unusually gifted craftsman who might, if he developed an original reading of life and a style peculiarly his own, become a poet of great distinction.

The too quickly following *Copper Sun* (1927) was almost totally mediocre. Except for the unusually complex dexterity of the close of "To Endymion" and the amusing irony, "More Than a Fool's Song," all of this volume consists of banal race poems or exercises in the imitation of Millay or Housman. *Ballad of the Brown Girl* (1927) was better, an expert retelling of one of the oldest ballads of race prejudice. *The Black Christ* (1929), Cullen's most ambitious volume to date, included a variety of metrical experiments (a tetrameter sonnet, a poem in dimeter), a number of poems in which an integrating figure controls the whole, an increasing number of poems that implemented his resolve to never let

> the clan
> Confine my singing to its ways
> Beyond the ways of man,

and a long narrative about a lynched Negro, who, like Christ, rises from the dead. Unfortunately, the lynch narrative seems strained—altogether inferior to Richard Wright's prose story, "Big Boy Leaves Home," for example—and the experiments are uniformly failures. The poems that do succeed continue to be occasional in substance, conventional in technique: "That Bright Chimeric Beast"; "At a Parting"; "Ghosts."

But *The Medea and Other Poems* (1935) promised again and more maturely. In the short poems that accompanied the (I have heard) mediocre translation, he developed a more complex and daring use of imagery than he had ever employed before. Such poems as "Only the Polished Skeleton" and "What I Am Saying Now Was Said Before" suggest that he had been reading older and modern metaphysical poets with great profit. But nobody noticed the development and this was the last volume of serious verse Cullen published during the eleven remaining years of his life. As his own selection, which contains all his best serious verse and too much that is mediocre or poor, evidences, he himself saw his career as a descending curve, for he chose twenty-five poems from *Color*, twenty-one, twenty-three, eighteen, and two poems from the volumes that followed it.

Harvey Curtis Webster, "A Difficult Career," *Poetry* 70, No. 4 (July 1947): 222–24

WILLIAM STANLEY BRAITHWAITE   Countee Cullen as a poet was a traditionalist in line with the great English poets, and an apostle of beauty with the fountainhead of his inspiration in the poetic philosophy of John Keats. If his imagination was scorched by the injustice and oppression of a people with whom his lot was thrown, like Keats whose sensitive nature was also wounded, he soared, not by way of escape, but by precept and counsel, into the abstract realm of the spirit. He caught the complexities and contradictions in the net of this idealism, as is attested to in this stanza from "More Than a Fool's Song"—

> The world's a curious riddle thrown
> Water-wise from heaven's cup;
> The souls we think are hurtling down
> Perhaps are climbing up.

No poet we have as yet produced was so complete and spontaneous a master of the poetic technique as Countee Cullen. His octosyllabic line has not been more skilfully handled by any modern poet. He has used the sonnet for many moods and themes and carved its fourteen lines of varied temper and structure with a lyrical unity that earns him a place in the company of Wordsworth, Rossetti and Bridges. He possessed an epigramatic gift and turn of wit that gave uncommon delight as witnessed in the series of "Epitaphs" among which the one "For a Mouthy Woman" is a masterpiece. His translations from Baudelaire, especially the sinuous felinity of cats, rank with those of Swinburne, Arthur Symons and George Dillon, in the rendering of that feverish and fantastic French poet into English. The fantasy of the "Wakeupworld" from the mythical narrative of "The Lost Zoo," established his poetic kinship in imaginative humor to the delightful foolery of Richard H. Barham's *Ingoldsby Legends*.

No one will deny that Countee Cullen escaped the aches that come to a sensitive spirit aware of racial prejudice and insult, but he did not allow them to distort or distemper the ideals and visions which endowed him as an artist and poet. He had as deep a sensibility for the human denials and aches which absorbed the lesser racial ones, and strove through the exquisite creation of imagery and music to evoke and communicate the spirit of Beauty as a solacing and restorative power. Time will, I think, accept him on the spiritual terms he set for himself in the poem "To John Keats, the Poet at Spring Time," and know that though he could sing a "Ballad for a Brown Girl" and make a "Litany of the Dark People" the blood and soul of mankind were alike in its passions and aspirations.

William Stanley Braithwaite, "On These I Stand," *Opportunity* 25, No. 3 (July–September 1947): 170

BLANCHE E. FERGUSON   Countee divided the book (*Copper Sun*) into five sections. The first part, called "Color," dealt with the emotions he felt as a Negro. He began with a ray of hope that promised:

> We shall not always plant while others reap
> The golden increment of bursting fruit, . . .

and he dedicated the poem, titled "From the Dark Tower," to Charles S. Johnson. Other verses portrayed vivid images—a colored blues singer, a proud black girl in her new red hat, a brown girl lovely and victorious in death.

The second section of *Copper Sun* bore the caption "The Deep in Love." Here the first poem, "Pity the Deep in Love," was inscribed to Fiona

Braithwaite. This young Bostonian was the daughter of William Stanley Braithwaite, himself a poet, but better known as editor of seventeen volumes of an anthology of American poetry spanning the years 1913 to 1929. Although his poem to Yolande dominated the love section in *Copper Sun*, other lyrics harped on the themes of unrequited love and faithless sweethearts.

The eight poems written in Mr. ⟨Robert⟩ Hillyer's class formed the third part of the volume. They were labeled simply "At Cambridge," and included the English verse forms that Cullen had learned to execute with competence. The section ended with "To Lovers of Earth, Fair Warning," the poem in rime royal that Hillyer later praised and quoted in his book.

There followed a variety of poems in Part Four titled "Varia." Here Cullen placed the four pieces he had composed during that memorable journey abroad with his father—the tributes to Shelley and Keats and his reactions to the city of Jerusalem and its Wailing Wall. Here too were his "Lines to My Father." There was also a stanza dedicated to Amy Lowell and one to John Haynes Holmes written for the Twentieth Anniversary Dinner given by a grateful community in honor of the celebrated preacher. (Dr. Holmes later wrote a touching letter of appreciation, saying the poem was "characteristic of your young genius and moved me greatly.")

Copper Sun ended with a group of seven poems under the caption "Juvenilia." These were products of Cullen's youth, some of them written during his high school days at Clinton.

Critical reaction to this volume, while generally favorable, did not measure up to that burst of acclaim that had greeted his first book, *Color*. But Countee was encouraged to read among the reviews a statement in *The Nation* that said in part, "Best of all he can forget that he is of the colored race and be just 'poet' most of the time."

> Blanche E. Ferguson, *Countee Cullen and the Negro Renaissance* (New York: Dodd, Mead, 1966), pp. 90–92

MARGARET PERRY   Countee Cullen was primarily a lyricist, influenced by romantic poets of the nineteenth and twentieth centuries. Keats was perhaps the poet he most admired; and his most characteristic lyrics show a penchant toward writing in the style of Housman, Millay, and Edwin Arlington Robinson. Jay Saunders Redding called him the Ariel of

Negro poets, one who "cannot beat the tom-tom above a faint whisper nor know the primitive delights of black rain and scarlet sun," a writer of "delightful personal love lyrics." Therefore, it is not surprising to note that, besides poems concerning the race problem, Cullen's other two most constant themes were love and death. Emanuel Eisenberg explicitly cited this tendency in Cullen's poetry when his second book, *Copper Sun*, appeared. Eisenberg wrote: "In his second volume . . . Countee Cullen reveals the fatal limitations which must always restrict his expression in poetry. One-third of his poems are concerned with race, another third with love, another with death."

Most of these thematic preoccupations, especially with love and death, were commented upon by an English writer ⟨Winifred Knox⟩ also, who stated that "his poetry belongs to that which takes for its themes the love of lovely things, and the poignant sorrow for their loss in death." ⟨. . .⟩

The poems of Countee Cullen concerning race could fill an adequate volume, for he was involved in expressing how it felt to be a Negro from the publication of his first book, *Color*, to the publication of his last (which had, among the unpublished poems, one entitled "A Negro Mother's Lullaby"). Yet he was, and probably still is, considered the least race-conscious of the Negro poets, although—as Charles Glicksberg pointed out—he will, ironically enough, be remembered for his poems which deal with race and/ or the race problem.

Margaret Perry, *A Bio-Bibliography of Countee Cullen 1903–1946* (Westport, CT: Greenwood Press, 1971), pp. 24–27

ALAN R. SHUCARD   The first relatively important poem Cullen composed was the long *Ballad of the Brown Girl*, published as a separate volume in 1927. He wrote it as a sophomore at New York University, and it won second prize in the national Witter Bynner poetry contest for undergraduates, an award by the Poetry Society of America. It is undisputably racial—in terms of the definition effective here, "black poetry." To begin with, Cullen failed to discover until much later that the term "brown girl" as it was used in the old English ballad upon which his version was based had no racial connotation at all, but was only a designation for a peasant girl. In the Cullen poem the love triangle of the original, a gory ballad in which the man and his two lovers all perish, is transformed so that the following occurs: a peer named Lord Thomas is in love with "the lily-white maid," an appellation used interchangeably with "Fair London" and "pride"—of all possible sections of the country—"of all the south." Prodded by his grasping mother, though, the white man chooses to marry instead "the dark Brown Girl who knows / No more defining name." This decision is taken solely for economic reasons and despite Lord Thomas's awareness that "bitter tongues have worn their tips / In sneering at her shame." After the white peer marries the Brown Girl for material gain, Fair London plays a scene at the reception during which she wears her bitter tongue berating miscegenation: "only the rose and the rosee should mate, / Oh, never the hare and the hound." True, the Brown Girl mortally stabs the lily-white maid, but only after her new white husband has failed to defend her against the verbal abuse; before this, she has succeeded in keeping "her passions underfoot / Because she comes of kings." The theme of high African lineage concealed by menial blacks in an ambient white environment ⟨. . .⟩ appears elsewhere in Cullen. Where Lord Thomas is slow to avenge the insult to his brown wife, he is unhesitatingly brutal in punishing the Brown Girl for the murder of the white one; he throttles her with her own long hair. Only his own death inevitably remains to be brought about, and the explicit moral is that because he has permitted his mother to convince him to barter "love / For gold or fertile land," he has brought disaster upon one and all. Of special interest here is that while the sacrifice of love for economics is important to the ballad, the racial dimension is measurable also: love, for the lord, is white, as he is; riches are personified in black, as are also the forces of passion and vitality (that is, Fair London is poor and insipid by comparison with the Brown Girl). At the end of the poem, "The Brown Girl sleeps at her true lord's feet, / Fair London by his side"—a noteworthy positioning of the two women in relation to the lord.

There is a group of racial sub-themes in Cullen directly suggested by *The Ballad of the Brown Girl* or related to the racial ideas found there. Arthur P. Davis long ago referred to Cullen's absorption with Africa as "the alien-and-exile theme," a useful expression in the examination of Afro-American literature. He defines the term well as "an implied contrast between the Negro's present state as an oppressed alien and that happy existence long, long ago in his native land." *Color*, Cullen's first volume and, in terms of critical acclaim and his own sensibility, his best, provides a number of representative poems that reflect many of the racial sub-themes. It is fair to say "representative" because even shortly before his death, as he selected the poems that he wished to be remembered by in the volume *On These I Stand*, Cullen chose an inordinately large number of poems from *Color*. Touching directly on the matter of African heritage alluded to in the case of the Brown Girl are such verses as "A Song of Praise" in which he describes his dark love, whose walk is the replica of a barbaric African dance, as more desirable than the reader's white one; "Fruit of the Flower," in which he speaks of racial memories; and notably "Atlantic City Waiter" and "Heritage." In the former, the waiter must disavow half his pride and wear an acquiescent mask, though his dexterity embodies the history of "Ten thousand years on jungle clues." The longer "Heritage" is an attempt to determine what Africa means to the speaker: finally, he realizes that it is his essential soul that must be suppressed in a civilization that is inimical to it. ⟨. . .⟩ In the very beat is the tension between the coolness of the civilization in which he must live externally and the smoldering racial force that Cullen believes he carries within.

Alan R. Shucard, *Countee Cullen* (Boston: Twayne, 1984), pp. 22–24

HOUSTON A. BAKER, JR.   The space ascribed to Cullen seems describable as a dimly lit and seldom-visited chamber where genteel souls stare forth in benign solicitude. Darwin Turner, for example, calls him "the lost Ariel," and Nathan Huggins speaks of Cullen clinging "quite tenaciously to the genteel tradition." Such phrases indicate only that Cullen did not march to the beat of the drummer who has "boomlay, boomlay, boomlayed" us into the 1970s. But critics are often embarrassed by the poet who is out of step with the age, as though someone had brought out a picture of a nonpartisan ancestor and shown it to their most committed colleagues. There follow tacit dismissals, vague apologies, and overweening defenses. ⟨. . .⟩

The mode, or preshaping impulse, of his work is in harmony with his overall conception of the poet as a man who dwells above mundane realities; for Cullen, the poet is the dream keeper, the "man . . . endowed with more lively sensibility, more enthusiasm and tenderness," the individual who is "certain of nothing but of the holiness of the Heart's affection and the truth of Imagination." These quotations from Wordsworth and Keats are descriptive; they capture in brief the a priori mandates of the romantic poet. In *"Cor Cordium,"* "To John Keats, Poet. At Springtime," "For a Poet,"

"To an Unknown Poet," and "That Bright Chimeric Beast," Cullen defines the poet as a creator of immortal beauty, a man still in harmony with the mysterious and the ideal in an age "cold to the core, undeified," a person who wraps his dreams in "a silken cloth" and lays them away in "a box of gold." Such an author is far removed from the ideal social artist and can hardly be compared to many of today's black artists, who compose as though our lived realities were contingent upon their next quatrain. What we have, then, is a difference not in degree but in kind. To apply the standards of a socially oriented criticism to Countee Cullen and dismiss him is to achieve no more than a pyrrhic victory. To expect the majority of his work to consist of the type of idiomatic, foot-tapping, and right-on stanzas that mark much of the work of Langston Hughes and Don Lee is not only naive but also disappointing. Moreover, to search always for the racial import in the writings of an artist who believed the poet dealt (or, at least, should be able to deal) above the realm of simple earthly distinctions is to find little. To examine the writings of Countee Cullen in detail, however, and attempt to understand both his aesthetic standpoint and the major ideas in his poetry is to move closer to an intelligent interpretation of both the man and the tradition to which he belongs. ⟨. . .⟩

Most often criticized is Cullen's choice of the romantic mode and his reliance on a long-standing poetical tradition. And if his detractors stuck to these charges, there would be little conflict. Most, however, go beyond them and assume that, say, Langston Hughes and Jean Toomer were more forthright, "modern," and independent than Cullen. To do so is to forget that the publication of Hughes's first book was contingent upon the kind offices of Vachel Lindsay, and that Toomer was—according to Marjorie Content Toomer—a man who disavowed all allegiance to the Black Renaissance. The artistic independence of the black author was an implied goal rather than a tangible fact of the Renaissance, and one suspects that Cullen was not the only author who told Hughes that he wanted to be just a writer, not a "Negro" writer.

Houston A. Baker, Jr., "A Many-Colored Coat of Dreams: The Poetry of Countee Cullen," *Afro-American Poetics: Revisions of Harlem and the Black Aesthetic* (Madison: University of Wisconsin Press, 1988), pp. 52–54, 59

GERALD EARLY   Perhaps Countee Cullen was never fully understood as a poet or a writer because he has never been understood fully as a man. There is, and always has been, a quality of unknowableness, sheer inscrutability, that surrounds Cullen and is no better symbolized, in a small yet telling way, than by the official, but varied accounts of his height. His passport of both 1934 and 1938 gives his height as 5′ 3″, his selective service registration card of 1942 lists him as 5′ 10″ and his war ration book number 3, issued when Cullen was forty years old, gives his height as 5′ 7″.

We still do not know where Cullen was born. In James W. Tuttleton's extremely useful essay "Countee Cullen at 'The Heights,' " which provides a detailed account of Cullen's undergraduate years at New York University, we learn that Cullen's college transcript, for which he himself provided the information, lists his place of birth as Louisville, Kentucky. This transcript was dated 1922. In the biographical headnote which Cullen wrote for his selections of poetry—contained in his own anthology of black poetry, *Caroling Dusk*—Cullen says he was born in New York City. ⟨. . .⟩ Whatever the reasons for Cullen changing the place of his birth, one inescapable fact is that in 1922 he was a relatively obscure but well-regarded black student with some poetic inclination and ability. By 1927 only Edna St. Vincent Millay surpassed him in American poetry circles in critical and press attention. Here with the whole business of birthplaces, we have the difference between the public and private Cullen. ⟨. . .⟩ Around the time of Cullen's death, stories began to circulate that he was born in Baltimore (one writer even says that Mrs. ⟨Ida⟩ Cullen confirms this). But there is little evidence for this ⟨. . .⟩ Oddly Beulah Reimherr, who had done the most extensive research into Cullen's childhood and young life, finds no record of anything about him in either the Louisville or Baltimore Bureau of Vital Statistics. There is, moreover, no birth record for Cullen in New York City. The mystery remains unsolved. ⟨. . .⟩

⟨. . .⟩ Cullen was very taken with the art of lying or why else did he have his cat tell tall tales in *The Lost Zoo* and in *My Lives and How I Lost Them*, or why else did he translate *The Medea*, which is all about the lying of two lovers, or why write a novel where the central character lies about his conversion? The entire scope of Cullen's 1930s career seems a long philosophical and aesthetic examination of the many creative and nefarious dimensions of lying, deception, and hypocrisy. Also the interest in lying as art explains the character Sam Lucas in *One Way to Heaven*. Many critics have felt that Cullen named the character Lucas because his own real name may have been Lucas. What makes a great deal more sense is that the con man character of Cullen's novel is named after the great black stage minstrel of the same name who was very popular in the early 1900s. As the novel turns on Lucas's ability to act, to play out a conversion that he does not feel convincingly, both in the beginning of the novel and at the novel's end, we see instantly that the book centers on the art of lying, and what black person was a better professional liar than a minstrel with his degrading, low, stereotypical comedy? In fact, the connection between the novel's character and the minstrel is made even more explicit by the symbols of the playing cards and razor, which Sam tosses away at every conversion. These are of course the props of the stereotypical black minstrel.

> Gerald Early, "Introduction," *My Soul's High Song: The Collected Writings of Countee Cullen, Voice of the Harlem Renaissance*, ed. Gerald Early (New York: Doubleday, 1991), pp. 6–8, 59

MICHEL FABRE   How can one evaluate the impact of French culture and Parisian life on the works of "the greatest francophile" of the Harlem Renaissance? Besides, how far did his presence in Paris help establish links between Afro-American writers and the French-speaking world? Clearly, Cullen spent nearly as much time in France as Claude McKay, and although his acquaintance was less diverse than McKay's and largely restricted to Paris, Cullen's knowledge of the language and culture enabled him to appreciate France far more than Hughes, and clearly as much as McKay, did. But differences in class and ideological choice intervened: whereas McKay was impatient with polished circles and the literati and seemed to breathe more freely among "the folks," Cullen gives the impression that he felt he was slumming when he made the rounds of working-class dance halls or tried the exotic setting of the Bal Colonial. He enjoyed these deeply, but possibly owing to his puritanical upbringing, one side of his personality would hold his spontaneity in check. Or, when attending a performance of *Rigoletto*, he would feel compelled to apologize for liking bel canto. He was visibly torn: he sought refinement but craved more vital, lusty entertainment than romantic infatuation. Thus France could quench his thirst for culture and unbridled enjoyment alike. Paris was the City of Light, the repository of ancient traditions, and also the embodiment of sexually free and piquantly dissolute life to which a touch of Africa or the West Indies added spice.

Cullen also visualized France as a generous mother-country. In America, which was his home, he felt that much was denied him because of his color. As a result he projected France as a haven, a substitute mother, as he made clear in his sonnet "To France":

> Among a fair and kindly foreign folk
> There might I only breathe my latest days,
> With those rich accents falling on my ear
> That most have made me feel that freedom's rays
> Still have a shrine where they may leap and soar—
> Though I were palsied there, or halt, or blind,
> So were I there, I think I should not mind.

Michel Fabre, *From Harlem to Paris: Black American Writers in France 1840–1980* (Urbana: University of Illinois Press, 1991), pp. 88–89

◈ *Bibliography*

Color. 1925.

The Ballad of the Brown Girl: An Old Ballad Retold. 1927.

Copper Sun. 1927.

Caroling Dusk: An Anthology of Verse by Negro Poets (editor). 1927.

The Black Christ and Other Poems. 1929.

One Way to Heaven. 1932.

The Medea and Some Poems. 1935.

The Lost Zoo (A Rhyme for the Young, but Not Too Young). 1940.

My Lives and How I Lost Them. 1942.

On These I Stand: An Anthology of the Best Poems of Countee Cullen. 1947.

My Soul's High Song: The Collected Writings of Countee Cullen, Voice of the Harlem Renaissance. Ed. Gerald Early. 1991.

Randolph Edmonds
1900–1983

SHEPPARD RANDOLPH EDMONDS was born in Lawrenceville, Virginia, on April 30, 1900, to George Washington and Frances Fisherman Edmonds. Both of Edmonds's parents were born into slavery but emancipated while still children. His schooling was scant and sporadic until he entered Saint Paul's Normal and Industrial School (now St. Paul's College) in Lawrenceville. After graduation from St. Paul's as valedictorian in 1921, Edmonds entered Oberlin College on a scholarship, which, however, did not entirely stave off his financial burdens. Edmonds was forced to work a number of odd jobs and even to take time off from school in order to support himself.

It was at Oberlin that Edmonds began to write plays. He helped organize the Dunbar Forum, which fostered discussions about creative writing and the theatre, and with its members Edmonds staged his first full-length play, *Rocky Road* (1926), and some of his shorter works. Edmonds graduated from Oberlin in 1926 with a B.A. in English Literature. Later that year he accepted a position at Morgan State College in Baltimore, Maryland. At Morgan, Edmonds taught English and drama and founded the Morgan Dramatic Club and, in 1930, the Negro Intercollegiate Drama Association. He spent the summers from 1927 to 1930 studying at Columbia University, where he received an M.A. degree in 1932.

Edmonds's busy academic life did not prevent him from working on his own writings. In 1930 he published his first collection of plays, *Shades and Shadows*. This volume contained six plays written during his days at Oberlin. The plays, according to Edmonds, were meant to be read aloud, not staged. His early dramas reflect his interest in folk plays, especially those of Paul Green.

In 1931 Edmonds married Irene Colbert, the great-granddaughter of abolitionist orator Henry Highland Garnett. They had two children, Henriette Highland Garnett and S. Randolph, Jr.

Edmonds's second collection, *Six Plays for a Negro Theatre*, appeared in 1934. Although dialect plays were falling out of favor with many black playwrights and their critics, all the plays in this volume are in dialect. Edmonds believed that great emotional effects could be achieved through the use of dialect.

From 1934 to 1935 Edmonds studied drama at Yale University under a fellowship from the Rockefeller Foundation. He then left Morgan to organize and head the Speech and Theatre Department at Dillard University in New Orleans, where he remained for the next twelve years. While at Dillard, Edmonds continued his efforts to popularize black theatre. In 1936 he organized the Southern Association of Dramatic and Speech Arts (SADSA), later renamed the National Association of Dramatic and Speech Arts (NADSA).

Edmonds's third collection, *The Land of Cotton and Other Plays*, appeared in 1942. This volume reflects his continuing interest in folk plays, but also a revival of his interest in "fantasy plays," somewhat stimulated by his studies at Dublin University and the London School of Speech and Dramatic Arts (made possible by a Rosenwald Fellowship awarded Edmonds in 1938). While in London, Edmonds attended the lectures of, and was introduced to, the great Irish playwright and fantasist Lord Dunsany. Edmonds's interest in fantasy can be seen most clearly in his attack on black historians in *The High Court of Historia* and in three later plays, *Simon in Cyrene* (1934), *The Shape of Wars to Come* (1943), and *Prometheus and the Atom* (1955).

Edmonds continued his efforts to develop and promote black theatre for the rest of his long life. In 1947 he joined the theatre arts department of Florida Agricultural and Mechanical University, remaining there until his retirement in 1970. In 1972 he was given a special citation from the American Theatre Association. In all, Edmonds wrote forty-eight plays, although several are still unpublished. He died on March 28, 1983.

◈ *Critical Extracts*

FREDERICK H. KOCH   The Negro has been struggling for a place in American culture. He has achieved distinction in poetry, in music, and in acting. Now he seems to be coming into his own in the theatre and in the drama.

Since Paul Green won the Pulitzer Prize in 1927 with his epic tragedy, *In Abraham's Bosom*, there has been a remarkable development in Negro theatre and the beginnings of an authentic Negro folk drama. After *Abraham* came DuBose and Dorothy Heyward's *Porgy*, representing a whole Negro neighborhood in Catfish Row, Charleston. As done by the New York Theatre Guild, this play proved to be a production of vivid, poetic quality. Then came *The Green Pastures* with its sensational run on Broadway and its triumphant tours of the country. And one of the most significant events of the New York season last year was a Negro folk-play written by a Negro, Hall Johnson, *Run Little Chillun*. It was hailed by the critics as a fresh native product. The wheel had come full circle. A native Negro drama, written by a talented Negro playwright, had arrived!

There is to-day a dramatic awakening among the young people of our Negro colleges and universities in the South toward a theatre and drama of their own people. Foremost, perhaps, in this new movement is Randolph Edmonds, teacher of English and dramatic director in Morgan College, Baltimore.

Last spring when I served as "critic judge" in the third annual tournament of The Negro Intercollegiate Dramatic Association in Richmond, I saw an exciting performance of Mr. Edmonds' folk-play of sawmill life, *Bad Man*, included in the present volume. I was much impressed with the enthusiasm, the freshness, and the imagination of the young playwright's work.

And no wonder. For Randolph Edmonds knows the life of the Negro; his parents were born slaves.

He himself was born in the little village of Lawrenceville, Virginia, in 1900. He attended country school in Brunswick County and later St. Paul's School there. Then he went away to Oberlin College where he was graduated in 1926, and to Columbia University where he received the Master's degree in 1932. He worked his way—on farms, in sawmill camps, hotels, factories, and on the railroad.

He tells me that at first he was interested in highly imaginative writing, but on reading Paul Green's *Lonesome Road* he became deeply interested in Negro peasant drama. The plays in this volume are the result. This is, as far as I know, the first volume of its kind. It suggests new horizons.

The new movement in the Negro colleges of the South promises much toward an authentic Negro drama.

Frederick H. Koch, "Foreword: The Negro Theatre Advancing," *Six Plays for a Negro Theatre* by Randolph Edmonds (Boston: Walter H. Baker Co., 1934), pp. 5–6

RANDOLPH EDMONDS   This volume of plays is intended primarily for use in Negro Little Theatres, where there has been for many years a great need for plays of Negro life written by Negroes. It is hoped, of course, that they will find their way into the repertory of other groups as well; for if plays are really worthwhile, they ought to contain some universal elements that will rise above the narrow confines of the nation or race of the cast of characters.

I am fully aware of the fact that there are many Negroes who do not like dialect plays. It has long been my opinion, however, that it is not the crude expressions of the peasant characters that contribute to this dislike; but rather the repelling atmosphere and the "psychology of the inferior" that somehow creep into the peasant plays of even the most unbiased authors of other racial groups.

In these plays, I have made an attempt to meet most of the usual objections raised against the dialect dramas with a combination of four elements that I explained somewhat at length in an article in one of our leading newspapers. They are worthwhile themes, sharply drawn conflict, positive characters, and a melodramatic plot.

It is hoped that a combination of these elements has resulted, on the negative side, in tragedies that are not too revolting in theme, and not too subtle and psychological in their action and exposition. On the positive side, the central characters have courage and conviction, and they fight heroically in their losing struggles. The melodramatic element is designed to make them dramatic enough to be understood and appreciated by the average audience rather than the sophisticated theatre-goer.

> Randolph Edmonds, "Preface," *Six Plays for a Negro Theatre* (Boston: Walter H. Baker Co., 1934), pp. 7–8

UNSIGNED   Much has been written about Negro life, some good, some very bad. A criticism of many characterizations of the Negro is that usually he is shown as a lying, stealing, gin-drinking, superstitious, cringing, crap-shooting person. He is usually the servile underdog, whose highest possibilities are those of a low-grade clown. These characterizations are emphasized on stage and screen because these are the popular conceptions, by some folk, of what the Negro really was and is. Mr. Edmonds dissents from this point of view and by so doing points the way to a new horizon in Negro drama. He fully realizes that there are some Negroes who may be typified by the descriptive terms above. He believes there are just as many Negroes who have a fuller, deeper appreciation of life values, who have convictions and who are willing to sacrifice their all for those convictions. This is the facet of Negro life which Mr. Edmonds seeks to portray in his *Six Plays for the Negro Theatre*.

The plays themselves show deep insight into Negro peasant life. They have atmosphere. The experiences of Mr. Edmonds in lumber camps, on the farm, in factories and the streets of Harlem are depicted in the characters which he created. But through it all the finer threads of life are interwoven. The first impression of *Bad Man* is that Thea Dugger is a hard, brutish, unprincipled animal. However, subsequent events show that Dugger, like most of us, has something fine under the exterior shell.

Breeders is woven around the most tragic theme of the slave era. Death is sweeter to a slave girl, than a life spent in breeding young slaves in a loveless marriage.

Nat Turner is an historical play built around the rebel and religious fanatic, Nat Turner. The courage and heroism and broad sympathies of the man give us a peep into the innermost thoughts of many slaves of the early 19th century.

An interesting and tragic conflict between the close-to-the-land Negro and the first generation "New Negro" is shown in *Old Man Pete*. The old parents, bred and born in the simple life, close to Nature and the Great Cause, cannot understand the frivolity and superficiality of the young people. Rather than undergo the slurs and denunciations of the children, particularly the in-laws, the old couple wander out on their way back to "Fuginia" and are frozen to death. Rather melodramatic, but effective.

Bleeding Hearts shows the hopelessness of the Negro tenant farmer. Held in peonage, sometimes worse than slavery, and experiencing all the hardships of the system, the share-cropper still nurses hope of a fuller, richer life.

The New Window is an excellent vehicle for portraying the superstitions of the Negro peasant as well as the sacrificing love of a Negro girl for her mother.

One weakness which may be noted in these plays is that dialect characters are sometimes allowed to shade off into very good English. They fall out of character by using a word or expression which the peasant would hardly have at his command. It is my view that this weakens several of the plays in spots. However, the situation can be overcome and is attributable to the difficulty, on the part of the author, of breaking through good English habits. However, the finished mechanical technique which Mr. Edmonds uses, his inclusiveness of view and his philosophy of life presage a brilliant career as well as lasting contributions to Negro dramatic art.

> Unsigned, [Review of *Six Plays for a Negro Theatre*], *Crisis* 41, No. 8 (August 1934): 246

BENJAMIN BRAWLEY   In 1930 he published *Shades and Shadows*, six stories in fanciful vein cast in dramatic form, influence coming from such authors as Maeterlinck and William Sharp. Not yet had he found his true bent, but he did so with *Six Plays for a Negro Theatre* (1934), a little book that must henceforth have high place in any study of the Negro drama. Said the author: "I am fully aware of the fact that there are many Negroes who do not like dialect plays. It has long been my opinion, however, that it is not the crude expressions of the peasant characters that contribute to the dislike, but rather the repelling atmosphere and the 'psychology of the inferior' that somehow creep into the peasant plays of even the most unbiased authors of other racial groups. . . . In these plays I have made an attempt to meet most of the usual objections raised against the dialect dramas with a combination of four elements that I explained somewhat at length in an article in one of our leading newspapers. They are worthwhile themes, sharply drawn conflict, positive characters, and a melodramatic plot." About the sharply drawn conflict and the positive characters there can be no doubt, but perhaps it is the melodramatic plot that Mr. Edmonds will want to watch. *Breeders*, for instance, the story of a young slave girl who is about to be forced into a union against her will, is especially violent in its action. The author shows to best advantage in *Bad Man*, a one-act play in which the Negroes working at a sawmill are accused of the murder of an old white man. When the mob forms, Thea Dugger, who all his life has been "a bad man, driftin' from one camp tuh another, shootin' and cuttin' and fightin'," becomes the hero, giving his life to save his friends. If Mr. Edmonds will refine his art and place less reliance on sensational effects, he will undoubtedly go far in his chosen field.

> Benjamin Brawley, *The Negro Genius* (New York: Dodd, Mead, 1937), pp. 285–86

RANDOLPH EDMONDS   We can conclude ⟨. . .⟩ that there will very likely be no truly great playwrights in our day and generation. If so, it will be contrary to what we may expect from the conclusions of dramatic history; for no country and no race has produced a supreme dramatist during their early years of experimentation with the theatre arts. At best the Negro playwrights of today are merely "university wits" preparing the way for the sepia Shakespeare of tomorrow. This should not deter us, however, from writing, producing, and publishing even though we realize that the best is yet to be.

It follows from all that has been said, that this volume makes no claim of being a collection of masterpieces since this is not to be expected of any Negro playwright of our time. This book is offered, however, because each play has been produced and has demonstrated beyond a doubt its ability to hold the interest of an audience despite the manifold shortcomings of the usual amateur acting and production. Is this not reason enough?

The Land of Cotton is a long play dealing with the system of tenant farming in the south. It is brutal and violent because all too often the system has been marked by such happenings. A conscious effort has been made to state the arguments of the landlords as well as those of the tenants; for the plantation owners do have a viewpoint that is all too often overlooked.

The play was begun in the playwriting class at Yale University in 1935 where I was in attendance on a fellowship granted by the General Education Board. Walter Prichard Eaton was the instructor. It was later finished and submitted for credit for the course. During 1938 two more revisions were made in Dublin, Ireland where I had gone to study amateur dramatic organizations on a fellowship granted by the Rosenwald Fund. It won first prize in a national playwriting contest sponsored by the Foundation of Expressive Arts in Baltimore, Maryland. It is designed for production more in the social theatres than in the university theatres.

Yellow Death, and *The High Court of Historia* were written for special Negro History Weekly productions. The first was written to point out the fact that the Negro has played a heroic part, even if it is only a small one, in the fight against the dreaded scourge of yellow fever. It is based upon a true historical episode.

The purpose of *The High Court of Historia* is quite obvious. It attacks the prevailing point of view taken by most Negro historians towards the teaching of Negro history. The play obviously does not read as well as it stages. The amateur director should be aware of the fact, however, that a play based on the court room trial technique rarely fails completely in the theatre. Costuming assumes an important part in this play as well as artificial movement and picturization.

Gangsters over Harlem is an obvious melodrama. It was written largely as an exercise in the technique of suspense and to illustrate the working of the "law of hospitality." It has had a wide demand in our Little Theatres with dozens of productions to its credit.

Silas Brown is a folk play. It is quite effective when folk characterizations are stressed.

The collection as a whole represents a contribution, however humble, to the growing list of plays so needed for production in Negro Little Theatres.

> Randolph Edmonds, "A Word on Plays and These Plays," *The Land of Cotton and Other Plays* (Washington, DC: Associated Publishers, 1942), pp. vi–viii

---

UNSIGNED   The play which gives its title to this volume was begun in the playwriting class in Yale University in 1935, when the writer was under the instruction of Walter Prichard Eaton; and, like the other four plays in this collection, it has demonstrated its ability to hold the interest of an audience. A Preface of marked modesty presents all five as a mere beginning of the dramatic production which may be looked for when Negro playwrights shall have concluded the early period of experimentation. Keeping in mind lessons learned from medieval days and from the ancient theater, the author focuses attention less on subtleties of character, psychological nuances and skillful handling of plots than upon broad characterizations and simple conflicts. In the maintaining of interest he has been successful. His work is realistic—in the sense that it is for sophisticated, mature readers.

> Unsigned, [Review of *The Land of Cotton and Other Plays*], *Catholic World* No. 947 (February 1944): 509

WILLIAM P. HALSTEAD and CLARA BEHRINGER   The efforts of one man, S. Randolph Edmonds, provided the stimulation for the organization of the Negro dramatic associations. It is noteworthy that he organized the first association a year before the National Theatre Conference was established.

On March 7, 1930, representatives from five colleges—Howard University, Hampton Institute, Morgan State, Virginia Union, and Virginia State Colleges—met on the Morgan campus at the invitation of Edmonds. These schools constituted the charter membership of the Negro Inter-Collegiate Dramatic Association. (The name was changed to Inter-Collegiate Dramatic Association in 1947.) Delegates elected Edmonds to the presidency, an office he retained for five years. Several college organizations applied for membership in the new association each year, but growth was slow. NIDA required that the member groups exchange plays, and distance between schools often prevented such exchange. After seven years the membership list included only ten schools. NIDA held annual conferences until World War II caused suspension of the meetings. President J. Newton Hill of Lincoln University and Secretary Felicia Anderson of Virginia State worked to keep the organization alive, and in 1946 regular meetings were resumed with one held at Bennett College.

Having removed to Dillard University at New Orleans, Edmonds founded the Southern Association of Dramatic Speech and Arts for schools of the southern area. Nineteen colleges and one community theatre responded to Edmonds' call for a meeting at Dillard, February 26–27, 1936.

Permanent organization was not attempted until the 1937 meeting at Florida A. and M. College. The charter member list included: Alabama State, Alcorn, Lane, LeMoyne, Morehouse, Morris Brown, Prairie View, Shorter, Spelman, Talladega, Tougaloo, Wiley, and Winston Salem State Teachers Colleges; Atlanta, Dillard, and Fisk Universities; and Tuskegee Institute. Edmonds was elected president. ⟨. . .⟩

Edmonds saw that almost every major area of study in the schools had its professional organization; specifically he noted that athletics had not attained its prominence through isolated intramural programs. Logically it followed that an intercollegiate association might stimulate interest in theatre. Further, Edmonds noted that as a result of shifting interest and personnel, few of the many community theatres which sprang up from time to time managed to achieve permanence. The stability and hardiness of college educational programs suggested that in this field might lie the hope of a continuing Negro theatre.

William P. Halstead and Clara Behringer, "National Theatre Organizations and Theatre Education," *History of Speech Education in America*, ed. Karl R. Wallace (New York: Appleton-Century-Crofts, 1954), pp. 648–50

FREDERICK W. BOND   In his *Bad Man*, Randolph Edmonds has chosen a shanty in a factory town for his locale. The inhabitants of the shanty are sawmill workers and their families, ranging from sincere Christians to hardened criminals of the gambling and habitually drinking type. Many of these hard-living characters are murderers and escaped convicts, illiterate, though possessed of keen, native wit. The hero, who is leader of a vicious gang, is one of this type. And to disobey one of his slightest whims swiftly results in death. Nothing seems to halt this tyrannical despotism, until a young, vivacious girl prevails upon him to prevent the slaughter of a member of a gang who has committed some trifling offense. Meanwhile, a mob of hoodlums forms to lynch a member of the group, who is supposed to have killed a white man. Then, refusing to believe that any of his gang is guilty, he attacks the mob single-handed, and, like a martyr in a great cause, meets his death.

For the unfortunately pathetic plight of "Old man Pete," the playwright has selected a neatly furnished apartment in Harlem for the scene of action. To this gay, Negro community of Manhattan Island, Old Man Pete Collier and his aged wife, by request, went to pay their children a visit. But soon after their arrival, the parents became aware that the children did not welcome their presence. As a matter of fact, the parents not only consumed food and bedroom space which were quite an economic item in New York, but they were actually a bore in the riotous and tumultuous life of Harlem. Recognizing the cold reception on the part of the children, the "ole folks" started for home with an insufficient amount of clothing or money for transportation. Incapable of standing the bitter cold of northern weather, their bodies were found frozen in a park the following morning.

In *Nat Turner* the dramatist is concerned with the reproduction of an historical incident in connection with the Southampton insurrectionist, who, in 1831, stirred a group of slaves to such a pitch of frenzy that they turned on their masters, slaying them and their families. In their attempt to throw off the shackles of slavery, by death and destruction of their tormentors, Nat Turner and his band were soon overtaken and put to death. The writing and subsequent production of *Nat Turner* won for Randolph Edmonds a scholarship at the Yale School of Drama in 1934.

Another drama, *Breeders*, the name of which suggests its theme, concerns itself with the raising of slaves in the same way in which hogs or cattle are produced. The master only wants healthy, fertile women to breed plenty of strong children to work on his plantation. Even though one of his female slaves is in love with a man of her own choice, the master tells her that she must marry another big, rough fellow forthwith. In her lover's anxiety to offset the impending forced marriage, he takes issue with the master and is slain. The maiden, in her bereavement over the death of her lover, drinks hemlock.

The most natural scene of *Bleeding Hearts*, a play of eight characters, also takes place on a southern plantation. The master insists that a mother and wife, living in one of his shanties, and who is desperately ill, come up to the Big House to help his wife. Later the husband finds a minister and a small group of friends praying and singing over her. In his bereavement, he not only curses the sympathizers but reproves God, who he thinks, if He really existed would have prevented his wife's dying.

The sixth and last of Randolph Edmonds' book of plays, *The New Window*, centers its theme on superstition. The heroine of the piece has certain superstitions which cause her to believe that bad luck will overtake her husband who earns his bread and butter by bootlegging. And strangely enough, as happens in all of Mr. Edmonds' plays, the hero meets with foul play.

Frederick W. Bond, *The Negro and the Drama* (Washington, DC: McGrath Publishing, 1969), pp. 125–27

HOLLIE I. WEST   As a college undergraduate in the early 1920s, Randolph Edmonds started writing plays to help fill the gaps in the small body of Afro-American dramatic literature.

Later, as a professor, he helped organize a consortium of black college drama groups and helped spearhead the black drama movement on university campuses.

His first wife, Irene Colbert Edmonds, now deceased, was also a drama professor, specializing in children's theater. And now his daughter, Henriette Highland Garnet Edmonds, is chairman of the Howard University drama department.

"We're a dramatic family," says his daughter. "Daddy would read Shakespeare to me when I was a child. Every now and then I'd get Little Red Riding Hood. My brother, Randolph, is an avid theatergoer even though he is a pediatrician."

The father recalls: "I used to read a chapter of *Alice in Wonderland* every night to Randolph when he was 5. He didn't understand it, but he wanted me to read it."

When Edmonds, 78, started teaching in 1926, the number of plays that portrayed blacks sympathetically was limited. "I wanted to do something about that," he says. "I worked with [historian] Carter Woodson on some things. We dramatized famous black characters."

During his years of teaching at Morgan State University, Dillard University and Florida A & M, Edmonds wrote 46 plays and 38 essays on drama and the humanities.

Looking back over more than half a century in drama, he's skeptical of the profanity and what he calls stereotypes in contemporary black drama.

"Out of 5,000 years of dramatic history, I don't know any that had bad language," he contends: "If we complain about stereotypes, we shouldn't create them."

Earlier in the week, he had lectured a Howard class about black dramatic stereotypes—the bad nigger, happy-go lucky male, oversexed female, pimps, drug addicts, prostitutes.

In the interview, he criticizes *The Toilet*, a play from the '60s by Amiri Baraka (formerly LeRoi Jones), for its obscene language. But, he says, "LeRoi Jones is the strongest dramatist that has come out of the last two decades."

His daughter, who is continuing the family drama tradition, has been department chairman at Howard since the summer of 1978 and has taught there for five years.

"We're still fighting some of the same problems that Daddy was fighting," she says. "We need more money. And we need a mass of educated people who feel that the arts are important."

Hollie I. West, "Updating Black Drama," *Washington Post*, 24 February 1979, p. C11

▣ *Bibliography*

Shades and Shadows. 1930.
Six Plays for a Negro Theatre. 1934.
The Land of Cotton and Other Plays. 1942.

Abram Hill
1910–1986

ABRAHAM BARRINGTON HILL was born in Atlanta, Georgia, on January 20, 1910. His father was a railroad fireman who moved his family to New York City in 1925. While attending Roosevelt and DeWitt Clinton high schools in New York, Hill worked as a photographer's assistant and wrote short stories and an unpublished novel. Upon graduation, he served as a drama coach to Harlem church groups and took premedical courses at the City College of New York before attending Lincoln University in Pennsylvania in 1934. Lincoln did not have a drama major at the time, so Hill graduated in 1937 with a bachelor's degree in English.

Hill worked as a drama director with a unit of the Temporary Emergency Relief Association in Long Island and joined the WPA Federal Theatre in 1938 as a playwright. While at the Federal Theatre, Hill worked on the Living Newspaper Unit, coauthoring with John Silvera a history of black life called *Liberty Deferred*. Unfortunately the Federal Theatre was shut down before the play could be produced. Unable to find work on Broadway, Hill worked with Harlem's Rose McClendon Players, which produced his comedy *On Striver's Row* in 1940. Hill was involved with the founding of the Negro Playwrights Company in 1940 but left the group early on, feeling that its members were too willing to sacrifice artistic quality for propaganda.

In 1940 Hill, along with Frederick O'Neal, founded the American Negro Theatre (ANT), an experimental theatre organization which attempted to portray black life realistically. Hill served as its artistic director and playwright in residence until he retired from theatre in 1948. ANT's first major production was Hill's *On Striver's Row,* which became one of their most popular attractions and was twice revived. In 1944 ANT produced Hill's adaptation of Philip Yordan's *Anna Lucasta*, a play originally about a Polish-American family that was extensively rewritten by Hill for a black cast. *Anna Lucasta* was an immediate hit, moving within weeks to a Broadway theatre and making instant stars out of many of its cast members. Unfortunately, the pressure on ANT to produce commercially successful plays, combined with the financial inexpertise of its members, greatly weakened the organization. Plays produced by ANT after *Anna Lucasta*, such as Hill's boxing drama *Walk Hard* (1944), adapted from Len Zinberg's novel *Walk Hard—Talk Loud*, were judged in terms of their potential success on Broadway, and after 1945 ANT produced only commercially "safe" plays written by white authors.

Hill left the organization in 1948, and after a moderately successful production of *The Power of Darkness*, his all-black adaptation of Leo Tolstoy's novel of the same name, he retired from theatre. Hill spent the rest of his life writing plays and articles, teaching, lecturing, consulting, and traveling. He died in New York on October 6, 1986, survived by his wife, Ruth Mueller Hill.

◈ *Critical Extracts*

L. C.   After several seasons of weighty theatrical fare, the American Negro Theatre last night turned its hand to comedy. It chose to do so with Abram Hill's *On Striver's Row*, a featherweight farce dealing with the social pretensions and middle-class snobbery up Harlem way. There is a good idea behind Mr. Hill's work, one which might have proved effective in the hands of an expert, but it is wasted by a general lack of cohesiveness in the plot. Probably the chief fault with the story is the need of a shrewd, sharp-cutting wit that usually is associated with successful satire. Notwithstanding, *On Striver's Row* proves that Harlem can laugh heartily at itself when the occasion warrants.

The action of the play takes place in the lavish apartment of the Van Strivens, located somewhere in the heart of Harlem. They are a socially conscious lot whose chief concern is to make the right impression and properly introduce their daughter to the correct circles. How a Brooklyn rival almost upsets their social plans and aspirations provides the chief basis of the comedy. Mr. Hill's characters, however, are of the stock variety and the plot somehow appears to move in no particular direction.

L. C., "Harlem Laughs at Itself," *New York Times*, 1 March 1946, p. 17

WOLCOTT GIBBS   With the exception of a foolish and quite unbelievable final curtain, the Broadway version of *Anna Lucasta*, at the Mansfield, is a dignified and often exciting enterprise. As you probably know, it is the story of a colored prostitute who lends herself to a scheme to marry a virtuous young Negro with eight hundred dollars, apparently a lot of money in a small town in Pennsylvania. She makes, however, the mistake of falling in love with him, and when her incestuous father exposes her past, she goes back to her old life rather than take the risk of jeopardizing her husband's career.

I didn't see the Harlem production, but I understand that up there the ending was tragic, culminating in Anna's suicide. For not entirely inscrutable reasons, it has been decided to end things happily at the Mansfield, with the hero and heroine reunited and all the other complications resolved in a neat manner, presumably very healthy at the box office. This is an error and a serious one, especially as it involves a curtain line that might seem coy even in *Peter Rabbit*, but in view of the excellence of the whole performance, I think it can be overlooked. ⟨. . .⟩

The all-colored cast, directed by Harry Wagstaff Gribble, is on the whole as good as it could possibly be, resisting what obviously must have been a considerable temptation to act all over the place. Hilda Simms, as Anna, has, of course, the biggest part and achieves a combination of abandon and pathos that seemed to me very impressive. Of the others, I admired Rosette LeNoire, Georgia Burke, Frederick O'Neal, and Canada Lee, who swaggers through a rather minor part with his usual authority and grace. If, in fact, I have any complaint to make, it might be that George Randol, as Anna's pathological pop, plays some of his scenes as they might conceivably have been done by Jimmy Savo, and Earle Hyman hasn't quite the presence or style you might expect in an actor who is supposed to be a great lover. Frederick Fox's domestic interior and Brooklyn bar gave me the horrors, which naturally is just exactly what they were supposed to do.

Wolcott Gibbs, "Bad Girl," *New Yorker*, 9 September 1944, p. 40

STARK YOUNG   For people who think that under given circumstances the Negro race is not different from the white, there is a clear enough approach to *Anna Lucasta*, the new play performed by an all-Negro company and the first play with which the American Negro Theatre earlier this season claimed public attention. By this approach we may state that this play is less tedious and fatuous than Maxwell Anderson's *Candle in the Wind* and has more narrative suspense, such as it is. It is less vulgarly pretentious than Lillian Hellman's *The Searching Wind*. It is less mature than these plays, and without the long theatre experience that underlies them.

As a play, however, *Anna Lucasta* is merely a vacantly written little melodrama about a fallen daughter kicked out on the streets by the harsh father, believed in by her mother, and brought home to be married off to the son of the father's friend, a young man with eight hundred dollars and in need of a wife. At first sight the two fall genuinely in love—via a wretched, unconvincing, stock-company scene. There are scenes in a bar, with another street-walker and sailor clients. The snow is falling outside. At the wedding Anna's past is betrayed by her father, she returns to the streets and the sailors, the bar, everything, in sum, and worse. The lover-husband remains constant and at the last snowy curtain the two are reunited.

The performances by the sizable company—most of whom are very nearly white—are no worse than we often see on Broadway. There is no training behind this acting or content about it. And there is the familiar lack of any method for the actor to go by; we have only personal exhibition and surface. With the exception of Mr. Canada Lee, whose part is too poorly written or conceived to give him much chance, there is in fact no acting to speak of at all, and no particular evidence of talent. Miss Hilda Simms in the full role of the heroine is ready enough but never moving or even faintly convincing.

On the basis of belief that there are certain qualities that, at present anyhow, are specially and highly characteristic of the Negro race, we may say that *Anna Lucasta* throws away most of the possibilities in rich, warm feeling, in vividness, in a sense of rhythmic movement and in the engaging and dramatic voices so often found among Negroes, all of which make such excellent stage material. In this play about Negroes the elements of imaginative speech and the subtleties of insight and quick responsiveness have not been discovered at all.

On one hand, to praise this occasion of *Anna Lucasta* merely because it is the work of Negro players needing encouragement, etc., may be well meant enough, but is only a form of condescension. On the other hand, there may be those who, for all their supposed Broadway, big-city sophistication, find that this sort of thing, falling snow and tripe, is just what they like.

Stark Young, "Anna Lucasta," New Republic, 18 September 1944, pp. 339–40

LOUIS KRONENBERGER   Adapted by the ANT's director, Abram Hill, from a novel by Len Zinberg, *Walk Hard* is a cruder and less absorbing play than *Anna Lucasta*, and has been given a considerably less effective production. But despite faults that pretty well wreck it as drama, a good deal of it is pretty lively theater. Even at its poorest, the ANT gets more punch into its productions than any other of our experimental theaters.

Walk Hard is the story of Andy Whitman, a young Negro who sees red at slurs against his race. Given a shot at a boxing career, he makes good progress until he arouses the hostility of a vicious big-shot promoter whom he defies and eventually slugs. It looks like curtains for his career, but at the end the author pulls a winning card from up his sleeve.

Superimposed on the story, which is conveyed in hard naturalistic terms, is a certain amount of symbolism about fighting evil, and a sudden perception on Andy's part of the right militant attitude—he has been showing the wrong one—for a Negro to maintain. But none of this really fuses with the story. It is introduced all too belatedly and overtly in a disastrous final scene that has nothing of the play behind it. The play seems headed for violence rather than vision. ⟨. . .⟩

The play suffers, too, from not having a sharp enough story line. It halts to indulge in too many scenes that exist for their own sake and introduces too many characters, even though a lot of them are interesting. Too often *Walk Hard* suggests its broad novelistic origin; too often, also, it falls down in the crucial matter of its writing.

But it does hold your interest, and does provide a number of crudely vigorous scenes. The best of these have to do with the grubby side of the fight world, with its punks and small-timers and has-beens; they are portrayed in tough language, with no holds barred. There are also some nice moments involving Andy's girl and his family. But *Walk Hard* never rises from effective scenes to an effective play.

Louis Kronenberger, "Pretty Faulty but not Dull," PM Daily, 1 December 1944, p. 20

MILES M. JEFFERSON   In a stuffy Harlem basement, the American Theater, under the tutelage of Abram Hill, tried out a play last summer that was later to create something of a furore downtown. Harry Wagstaff Gribble, a white director of some eminence, was invited to lend his hand at steering this play with his skill and experience. The play was Philip Yordan's *Anna Lucasta*, in the beginning concerned with a Polish prostitute and her life torments and maladjustments. The transition of Anna from Pole to Negro was made, apparently, without much perspired effort, and with no racial prejudice.

The play was presented in Harlem for about six weeks during June and July. This reporter enjoyed the happy experience of making the acquaintance of Anna uptown when she was gloomy and tragic, but beguiling and arresting, before she decided life was a gamble and danced downtown to exhibit herself as a more cheerful butterfly at the Mansfield Theater on Forty-seventh Street.

Comparisons are inevitable and even pertinent. Uptown the play was rough and unpolished, but somehow vital and insistent. Its plot was a "ten-twen'-thirt' " melodramatic carbon copy of *Anna Christie*, plus a plentiful sprinkling of the clichés of the small-town-girl-good-at-heart-gone-wrong. White Hope appeared in the guise of the young son of a family friend who emerged from the South in search of a wife and found Anna, and for a while all seemed destined for happiness until Anna's father, in a moment of pale-tinted incestuous desire, interfered and sent his daughter back in disillusionment to her Brooklyn beat and eventual suicide.

This certainly was a far from profound or novel story to tell, but the infectious enthusiasm of a little group of unknown Negro actors in Harlem imbued the tawdry little play with so much vigor and raw life that you sat on uncomfortable camp chairs until the final rickety curtain, and you came out of a spell only created by real theater when it was all over. *Anna Lucasta* as presented in Harlem was one of those miracles that makes the theater so unpredictable, and, consequently, so irresistible. ⟨. . .⟩

Though still lively theater, *Anna* downtown is a more superficial girl than she was in the Harlem basement. There she was an earnest, genuinely tormented, a tragic figure, if a melodramatic one. Her family, responsible for much of her misery, was seen clearly and believably in Harlem through a mirror thrown clairvoyantly up to Nature; on Broadway it is still a human clan of misfits of different sizes and dimensions, intensities and foibles, geared for laughs. The play was rewritten for laughs in order, it is presumed, to make it a palatable commodity downtown; uptown it stuck close to reality. Anna downtown doesn't end it all at the final curtain, but answers the call of her persistent lover who is standing in the snow outside a stagey door (yes, even the driven snow from *Uncle Tom's Cabin* is on hand!) with "I'm coming, Snow-man" or something similar to such hammy coyness.

Downtown it is the same finely blended acting of an earnest and extremely able cast that must be responsible for the success of the play. Otherwise a drama so audaciously maudlin in essence, and so hackneyed in plot could not make its way on Broadway, even though it must be admitted that ham thinly sliced is ever so often marketable there. White reviewers gave much publicity to the discovery that the play was, to quote Mr. Kronenberger of *PM*, "not about Negroes but about people. The characters transcend their race and its special problems to become human creatures, to suggest anybody's family."

Miles M. Jefferson, "The Negro on Broadway—1944," *Phylon* 4, No. 1 (First Quarter 1945): 50–51

LEWIS NICHOLS   The American Negro Theatre, whence sprang *Anna Lucasta*, is turning its attention these evenings to another play it hopes may wander down town from 135th Street. It is *Walk Hard*, by Abram Hill, director of the theatre, and after an opening a couple of weeks ago, it invited a few Broadway friends for a formal visit last night. The new play unfortunately is no *Anna Lucasta*, although it does have its moments, and, like most of the American Negro Theatre's productions, it is played for as much excitement as the traffic will bear. Harlem at curtain time never is a dull place, and the enthusiasm the cast brings to *Walk Hard* manages at least part of the time to cover the fact that it is not a particularly good play.

Mr. Hill based his drama on *Walk Hard—Talk Loud*, by Len Zinberg. Its central character is a young prize fighter, who battles his way up toward the championship at the same time he battles against prejudice. Mr. Hill's central theme is legitimate and important, but he introduces a number of extraneous scenes and people which slow his play and cloud his story. The actors never are slow, however, for when 135th Street is dealing with fighters, it hits hard; the punches delivered on the small stage of Harlem would kill actors down the road. ⟨. . .⟩

While *Walk Hard* is not of the quality of *Anna Lucasta*, it is considerably above most plays being tried out in the byways of the city.

Lewis Nicols, "Boxer's Rebellion," *New York Times*, 1 December 1944, p. 28

MILES M. JEFFERSON   Mr. Abram Hill, free to try his hand at anything striking his fancy, since he was no longer director of the destinies of ANT, tackled the production of his own adaptation of Tolstoy's *The Power of Darkness*, made available for examination at the Master Institute. A group of actors from the organization with which he was formerly associated suffered all kinds of aches and pains without notable success. Any adaptation of Tolstoy's philosophical study of sacred and profane passions and torments would require deep and searching analytical skill not apparent in Mr. Hill's translation. Besides, the play is so intrinsically Slavic in its original form that its racial subtleties would be extremely difficult, if not impossible to capture by an alien troupe of actors. The bitter, intractable nature of the Russian spirit, no time more manifest than today in our dealings with it, defies transfer to a town in the American South.

Miles M. Jefferson, "The Negro on Broadway—1948–1949," *Phylon* 10, No. 2 (Second Quarter 1949): 108–9

DORIS E. ABRAMSON   ⟨. . .⟩ a Living Newspaper about Negro life in America was written by two Negro playwrights, John Silvera and Abram Hill. It was entitled *Liberty Deferred* and was publicized but never produced. ⟨. . .⟩

In a brief prepared by the Negro Arts Committee of the Federal Arts Council, a number of citizens—including ministers, labor leaders, both Negro and white artists, librarians, theatre committees—criticized the Federal Theatre for not producing *Liberty Deferred*, in fact for not doing more for Negro playwrights in general. Too few plays about Negroes, according to this committee, were outside the Broadway pattern: "The novelty of 'swinging' the classics does not cover the field. New Negro plays will be needed, and the Negro playwright is the logical one to write them." Plays by Negroes had been acclaimed worthwhile for production, they went on, but then were lost in red tape.

Part of a review by Dan Burley, drama critic for the *Amsterdam News,* was quoted in brief:

> The Negro according to *Liberty Deferred* is, has, and may be expected to be a victim of oppression because of his place on the economic ladder.—Done in the best living-newspaper manner, *Liberty Deferred* presents its history through the eyes of its authors.—I believe the authors have assembled a singularly thought-provoking piece of propaganda and a valuable contribution to Negro literature.

The committee contended that authors Silvera and Hill had been waiting for six months for action to be taken on their play by the New York City Federal Theatre Planning Board. "And this play but illustrates the fate of numerous worthy Negro plays by Negro playwrights."

These were serious charges, and they were answered by Emmet Lavery, director of the National Service Bureau. In his letter to the committee he stated that he had originally had great hopes for this Living Newspaper about Negroes, but when he read the completed script he "felt definitely that it did not bear out the high hopes I had for it." His letter concluded with a statement of concern for the development of Negro drama and the hope that he had for a Negro trilogy being written by Hughes Allison. The trilogy has never appeared; *Liberty Deferred* has only recently turned up at the Lincoln Center Theatre Collection.

Doris E. Abramson, *Negro Playwrights in the American Theatre 1925–1959* (New York: Columbia University Press, 1967), pp. 65–66.

LANGSTON HUGHES and MILTON MELTZER   ⟨. . .⟩ in the basement of a public library, the American Negro Theatre directed by Abram Hill came into being, and its acting group included Sidney Poitier and Harry Belafonte, who there developed their burgeoning talents in plays by or about Negroes. However, the theatre's only production that went from Harlem to Broadway was not a play of Negro life at all, but a comedy by Philip Yordan about a Polish family, adapted for performance by colored actors. The American Negro Theatre's presentation of *Anna Lucasta,* with Hilda Simms as Anna, opened uptown. It was such a hit in Harlem that it was taken to Broadway in 1944 where it ran for almost three years, chalking up 957 performances. Another company played for forty weeks in Chicago, and a third toured New England. *Anna Lucasta* years later was made into a motion picture—in fact, two pictures—one with a white cast including Paulette Goddard, and subsequently a second film with a Negro cast starring Eartha Kitt. Unfortunately, commercial success in the long run did not do the American Negro Theatre any lasting good. The group consciously began to aim its uptown productions at downtown consumption, thereby losing its ethnic touch as well as its community audience. It soon fell apart. Since that group there has been nothing like it in Harlem for the development of either actors or playwrights.

> Langston Hughes and Milton Meltzer, "Drama in Harlem," *Black Magic: A Pictorial History of the Negro in American Entertainment* (Englewood Cliffs, NJ: Prentice-Hall, 1967), p. 125

LOFTEN MITCHELL   At the heart of Abe's play ⟨*On Striver's Row*⟩ is the Van Striven family. They are black and they are very middle-class. Striver's Row is, of course, that beautiful group of houses on 137th Street, 138th Street and 139th Street, built by architect Stanford White. Writers—that is, well-paid writers—doctors, lawyers, dentists and other black and a number of white professionals live there as of this writing. But you have to strive to live on Striver's Row.

And the Van Strivens are striving. Dolly, the wife of Mr. Van Striven, is the declared leader of her social set. She gives her daughter a big coming-out party. Well, Mrs. Envy is Dolly's rival in this social set and she wants to break up the party and embarrass Dolly. So Mrs. Envy invites Joe Smothers, a jive-talking, hip character, to break up the party. The joint begins to jump as Joe carries on. He puts down some long Harlem talk. He has brought along a broad named Ruby and they begin to Lindy Hop and tear up the house.

Dolly is about to faint, but her maid from the country saves the day. She recognizes Joe Smothers and well she should, because she asks: "Honey, are those the new clothes I bought for you?" All Joe can say is "Damn Sam!" Furthermore, Joe is in hot water because he has Ruby there. He must confess to the maid that he is doing all of this for her because Mrs. Envy has paid him to break up Dolly's party. Joe and Ruby get out of there in a hurry because Dolly has her shoe off. As the second act curtain falls, Dolly has raised her shoe to Mrs. Envy's head, declaring:

"I am going to put some misery where it belongs!"

This is really an injustice to Abe Hill's play. You laugh, but you have tears in your eyes because he also deals with the black country maid who came north to be treated well by whites and blacks. And she is painfully hurt.

Few are the people who know enough to appreciate Abe Hill's marvelous play. Many a good, honest white critic has stubbed his toe trying to analyze the play. Ditto many black critics. I have only seen it six times so I am, of course, prejudiced in my point of view. ⟨. . .⟩

This tall, gentlemanly scholar was prematurely bald. He had too much intelligence for hair to stay on his head. I truly admired and still admire Abe. He sacrificed having a family and poured everything he had into the building of an American Negro theatre in the Harlem area. And he had his heart broken.

For many people—big people and little people—went after Abe's head. Beloved friends began to ask him why he was famous and not rich. The pressure mounted, increasingly. No one bothered to look at his record: All he did was to found a theatre, sacrifice his writing career and his potential family for that cause, promote present-day stars like Sidney Poitier and Hilda Simms and Harry Belafonte, and such writers as Alice Childress. Many brought stories to me and I told them to go to hell. I was not going to get in the middle of downright jealousy. I despise small-minded people of all nations, races and creeds.

> Loften Mitchell, "A Voice: Abram Hill," *Voices of the Black Theatre* (Clifton, NJ: James T. White, 1975), pp. 113–15

ABRAM HILL   I have not really been active in the theatre in almost twenty years. I call myself divorced from the theatre, but about two or three times a year my good friend, Loften Mitchell, tries to draft me back into the business. I took a cue from him some years ago when I invited him out to speak to a group, Workshop 59, I was directing in Springfield Gardens, Long Island, and he said—among other things—to the students: "Theatre is a jealous mistress. She will totally absorb you."

I began to realize how much I had been really involved in being absorbed in theatre, and I finally concluded that she is a jealous "bee"—and I don't have to tell you what that means.

In June, 1940, a group of us got together and organized the American Negro Theatre. There were many unusual things about that theatre, but I believe the unique thing was that we were probably the only theatre group in history that had to rehearse in a funeral parlor, because there wasn't any free space anywhere else in the community. ⟨. . .⟩

Despite the pitfalls that threatened and sometimes destroyed group practice at every turn, the A.N.T heaved, wiggled and shook itself into a respectable experimental theatre. Attribute this to preparation. A.N.T. was not a group of black dilettantes dabbling on the periphery of sound theatre craft. Years of research, surveys, and the solutions to the problems inherent in this kind of activity predated the founding of the group. Ensemble playing, attuned almost in a musical manner; perfectionism in lieu of professionalism; thinking, artistic acting instead of the primitive natural; the development of supporting and responsive audiences were the ingredients that sparked critic John Chapman to tag A.N.T. as having: "The finest ensemble acting in town." ⟨. . .⟩

Among the foremost aims was to destroy the black stereotypes. As one of its early members, Ruby Dee was the personification of this aim. She was unique, but so was her opponent—the eyeball-rolling, ghost-frightened pickaninny. I say unique, because in modern times it has been taken for granted that the actor on the stage was the equal of the member of the audience.

May I digress for a moment? May I read from a piece I wrote a while back? "All our arts—and particularly the theatre—have been infected by attitudes that were firmly established by chattel slavery. The theatre took over and encouraged the idea of an inferior group of people. Under the institution of slavery, one of the onerous tasks of the enslaved people was that of entertaining their masters. Southern planters were proud of their black slaves who could dance and sing, pick the guitar, clap bones, and sometimes play the violin. It is understandable that the minstrel show became an established entertainment in the American theatre, perpetuating in dramatic form the cruel notion of race inferiority. For the minstrel show was a unique form of theatre, in which the actors were inferior to the members of the audience. The minstrel show waned, unlamented, but the stereotype persisted in the forties, and substantial vestiges are still with us today—witness some black stylized and unreal characterizations—bad English, propensity for big words, and glut that erodes some revival scenes.

"Contravening the stereotype is the portrayal of individual character, with all the color, variety, dignity, pettiness, virtue and evil, and incredibly complex and contradictory motives that the individual is possessed of—whatever his complexion. Many black players bathe comfortably in any roles that they are fortunate enough to get. However, any honest and moderately serious actor-artist can tell you that this problem—the problem of assessing and portraying human character in relation to *his heritage and environment*—is the problem that obsesses his waking hours and haunts his dreams."

> Abram Hill, "The Words of Abram Hill," *Voices of the Black Theatre*, ed. Loften Mitchell (Clifton, NJ: James T. White, 1975), pp. 117, 119–21

◈ *Bibliography*

Published Plays:

On Striver's Row. 1940 (produced). In *Roots of Black Drama*, ed. James V. Hatch and Lee Hamalian (1989).

Anna Lucasta. 1944 (produced). In *The Best Plays of 1944–45* (1945).

Walk Hard. 1944 (produced). In *Black Theater, U.S.A.*, ed. James V. Hatch (1974).

Split Down the Middle. 1970.

Plays Written and/or Produced But Not Published:

Stealing Lightning. 1937.

So Shall You Reap. 1937.

Hell's Half Acre. 1938.

Liberty Deferred. 1938.

Latin, Greek or Grits. 1939.

The Power of Darkness. 1948.

Miss Mabel. 1951.

Beyond the Bush. 1970.

Langston Hughes
1902–1967

JAMES LANGSTON HUGHES was born in Joplin, Missouri, on February 1, 1902. His mother, Carrie Langston Hughes, had been a schoolteacher; his father, James Nathaniel Hughes, was a storekeeper. James left for Mexico while his son was still an infant, and the latter was raised mostly by his grandmother, Mary Langston. Hughes lived for a time in Illinois with his mother, who remarried, and went to high school in Cleveland. He spent the summer of 1919 in Mexico with his father, then taught for a year in Mexican schools. He entered Columbia University in September 1921, a few months after his poem "The Negro Speaks of Rivers" appeared in the *Crisis* for June 1921.

After a year of schooling, Hughes took on various jobs in New York, on transatlantic ships, and in Paris. He returned to America in 1925, and while working as a busboy in Washington, D.C., he slipped three poems beside Vachel Lindsay's plate. Lindsay was impressed and began promoting the young poet. In 1925 Hughes won a literary contest in *Opportunity*, and his writing career was launched. His first collection of poems, *The Weary Blues*, was published in 1926. Another volume, *Fine Clothes to the Jew*, appeared the next year. A benefactor sent Hughes to Lincoln University, from which he received a B.A. in 1929.

Hughes subsequently supported himself as a poet, novelist, and writer of stories, screenplays, articles, children's books, and songs. His first novel, *Not without Laughter*, appeared in 1930. His first short-story collection was *The Ways of White Folks* (1934). He wrote a children's book in collaboration with Arna Bontemps, *Popo and Fifina, Children of Haiti* (1932), based on a trip Hughes took to Haiti in 1931. He also collaborated with Zora Neale Hurston on a folk comedy, *Mule Bone*, but it was not published until 1991.

Having received several literary awards and fellowships in the 1930s, including a Guggenheim Fellowship in 1935, Hughes was able to write without financial worries. He promoted black theatre in both Harlem and Los Angeles, and himself wrote a number of plays, the most famous of which is *Tambourines to Glory* (1958). In 1940 he published his first autobiography, *The Big Sea.*

Hughes moved to California in 1939, settling in Hollow Hills Farm near Monterey. Two years later he moved to Chicago, and from 1942 onward he lived in Harlem. Such volumes as *Shakespeare in Harlem* (1942) and *Fields of Wonder* (1947) established him as the leading black poet in America. Hughes's Communist leanings, initially triggered by a trip to the Soviet Union in 1931, caused him to be summoned before the House Un-American Activities Committee (HUAC), where, fearful of being imprisoned or black-balled, he repudiated any Communist or socialist tendencies and maintained that his repeated calls for social justice for black Americans, expressed in his earlier work, were not incompatible with American political ideals.

In the 1950s and 1960s, Hughes gained popularity through the recurring protagonist of his stories, Jesse B. Semple, or "Simple." These stories were collected in four volumes: *Simple Speaks His Mind* (1950), *Simple Takes a Wife* (1953), *Simple Stakes a Claim* (1957), and *Simple's Uncle Sam* (1965). A selection, *The Best of Simple,* appeared in 1961. Story collections not involving Simple are *Laughing to Keep from Crying* (1952) and *Something in Common and Other Stories* (1963). A second autobiography, *I Wonder as I Wander,* was published in 1956.

In his later years Hughes devoted himself to promoting black literature by compiling anthologies of black American poetry, fiction, and folklore, and by writing nonfiction books for children, including *The First Book of Negroes* (1952), *The First Book of Jazz* (1955), and *The First Book of Africa* (1960). He received the NAACP's Spingarn Medal in 1960 and was elected to the National Institute of Arts and Letters in 1961. Hughes never married. He died of congestive heart failure in New York City on May 22, 1967.

▨ *Critical Extracts*

LANGSTON HUGHES   ⟨. . .⟩ there is, for the American Negro artist who can escape the restrictions the more advanced among his own group would put upon him, a great field of unused material ready for his art. Without going outside his race, and even among the better classes with their "white" culture and conscious American manners, but still Negro enough to be different, there is sufficient matter to furnish a black artist with a lifetime of creative work. And when he chooses to touch on the relations between Negroes and whites in this country with their innumerable overtones and undertones, surely, and especially for literature and the drama, there is an inexhaustible supply of themes at hand. To these the Negro artist can give his racial individuality, his heritage of rhythm and warmth, and his incongruous humor that so often, as in the Blues, becomes ironic laughter mixed with tears. But let us look again at the mountain.

A prominent Negro clubwoman in Philadelphia paid eleven dollars to hear Raquel Meller sing Andalusian popular songs. But she told me a few weeks before she would not think of going to hear "that woman," Clara Smith, a great black artist, sing Negro folksongs. And many an upper-class Negro church, even now, would not dream of employing a spiritual in its services. The drab melodies in white folks' hymnbooks are much to be preferred. "We want to worship the Lord correctly and quietly. We don't believe in 'shouting.' Let's be dull like the Nordics," they say, in effect.

The road for the serious black artist, then, who would produce a racial art is most certainly rocky and the mountain is high. Until recently he received almost no encouragement for his work from either white or colored people. The fine novels of Chesnutt go out of print with neither race noticing their passing. The quaint charm and humor of Dunbar's dialect verse brought to him, in his day, largely the same kind of encouragement one would give a sideshow freak (A colored man writing poetry! How odd!) or a clown (How amusing!).

The present vogue in things Negro, although it may do as much harm as good for the budding colored artist, has at least done this: it has brought him forcibly to the attention of his own people among whom for so long, unless the other race had noticed him beforehand, he was a prophet with little honor. I understand that Charles Gilpin acted for years in Negro theaters without any special acclaim from his own, but when Broadway gave him eight curtain calls, Negroes, too, began to beat a tin pan in his honor. I know a young colored writer, a manual worker by day, who had been writing well for the colored magazines for some years, but it was not until he recently broke into the white publications and his first book was accepted by a prominent New York publisher that the "best" Negroes in his city took the trouble to discover that he lived there. Then almost immediately they decided to give a grand dinner for him. But the society ladies were careful to whisper to his mother that perhaps she'd better not come. They were not sure she would have an evening gown.

The Negro artist works against an undertow of sharp criticism and misunderstanding from his own group and unintentional bribes from the whites. "O, be respectable, write about nice people, show how good we are," say the Negroes. "Be stereotyped, don't go too far, don't shatter our illusions about you, don't amuse us too seriously. We will pay you," say the whites. Both would have told Jean Toomer not to write *Cane*. The colored people did not praise it. The white people did not buy it. Most of the colored people who did read *Cane* hate it. They are afraid of it. Although the critics gave it good reviews the public remained indifferent. Yet (excepting the work of Du Bois) *Cane* contains the finest prose written by a Negro in America. And like the singing of Robeson, it is truly racial. ⟨. . .⟩

Let the blare of Negro jazz bands and the bellowing voice of Bessie Smith singing Blues penetrate the closed ears of the colored near-intellectuals until they listen and perhaps understand. Let Paul Robeson singing Water Boy, and Rudolph Fisher writing about the streets of Harlem, and Jean Toomer holding the heart of Georgia in his hands, and Aaron Douglas drawing strange black fantasies cause the smug Negro middle class to turn from their white, respectable, ordinary books and papers to catch a glimmer of their own beauty. We younger Negro artists who create now intend to express our individual dark-skinned selves without fear or shame. If white people are pleased we are glad. If they are not, it doesn't matter. We know we are beautiful. And ugly too. The tom-tom cries and the tom-tom laughs. If colored people are pleased we are glad. If they are not, their displeasure doesn't matter either. We build our temples for tomorrow, strong as we know how, and we stand on top of the mountain, free within ourselves.

Langston Hughes, "The Negro Artist and the Racial Mountain" (1926), *Langston Hughes Review* 4, No. 1 (Spring 1985): 2–4

ALAIN LOCKE   Fine clothes may not make either the poet or the gentleman, but they certainly help; and it is a rare genius that can strip life to the buff and still poetize it. This, however, Langston Hughes has done, in a volume ⟨*Fine Clothes to the Jew*⟩ that is even more starkly realistic and colloquial than his first,—*The Weary Blues*. It is a current ambition in American poetry to take the common clay of life and fashion it to living beauty, but very few have succeeded, even Masters and Sandburg not invariably. They get their effects, but too often at the expense of poetry. Here, on the contrary, there is scarcely a prosaic note or a spiritual sag in spite of the fact that never has cruder colloquialism or more sordid life been put into the substance of poetry. The book is, therefore, notable as an achievement in poetic realism in addition to its particular value as a folk study in verse of Negro life.

The success of these poems owes much to the clever and apt device of taking folk-song forms and idioms as the mold into which the life of the plain people is descriptively poured. This gives not only an authentic background and the impression that it is the people themselves speaking, but the sordidness of common life is caught up in the lilt of its own poetry and without any sentimental propping attains something of the necessary elevation of art. Many of the poems are modelled in the exact metrical form of the Negro "Blues," now so suddenly popular, and in thought and style of expression are so close as scarcely to be distinguishable from the popular variety. But these poems are not transcriptions, every now and then one catches sight of the deft poetic touch that unostentatiously transforms them into folk portraits. ⟨. . .⟩ The author apparently loves the plain people in every aspect of their lives, their gin-drinking carousals, their street brawls, their tenement publicity, and their slum matings and partings, and reveals this segment of Negro life as it has never been shown before. Its open frankness will be a shock and a snare for the critic and moralist who cannot distinguish clay from mire. The poet has himself said elsewhere,—"The 'low-down' Negroes furnish a wealth of colorful, distinctive material for any artist, because they hold their individuality in the face of American standardizations. And perhaps these common people will give to the world its truly great Negro artist, the one who is not afraid to be himself." And as one watches Langston Hughes's own career, one wonders.

Alain Locke, "Common Clay and Poetry," *Nation*, 9 April 1927, p. 712

JAMES BALDWIN   Every time I read Langston Hughes I am amazed all over again by his genuine gifts—and depressed that he has done so little with them. A real discussion of his work demands more space than I have here, but this book ⟨*Selected Poems* (1959)⟩ contains a great deal which a more disciplined poet would have thrown into the waste-basket (almost all of the last section, for example).

There are the poems which almost succeed but which do not succeed, poems which take refuge, finally, in a fake simplicity in order to avoid the very difficult simplicity of the experience! And one sometimes has the impression, as in a poem like "Third Degree"—which is about the beating up of a Negro boy in a police station—that Hughes has had to hold the experience outside him in order to be able to write at all. And certainly this is understandable. Nevertheless, the poetic trick, so to speak, is to be within the experience and outside it at the same time—and the poem fails. ⟨. . .⟩

Hughes, in his sermons, blues and prayers, has working for him the power and the beat of Negro speech and Negro music. Negro speech is vivid largely because it is private. It is a kind of emotional shorthand—or sleight-of-hand—by means of which Negroes express, not only their relationship to each other, but their judgment of the white world. And, as the white world takes over this vocabulary—without the faintest notion of what it really means—the vocabulary is forced to change. The same thing is true of Negro music, which has had to become more and more complex in order to continue to express any of the private or collective experience.

Hughes knows the bitter truth behind these hieroglyphics: what they are designed to protect, what they are designed to convey. But he has not forced them into the realm of art where their meaning would become clear and overwhelming. "Hey, pop! / Re-bop! / Mop!" conveys much more on Lenox Avenue than it does in this book, which is not the way it ought to be.

Hughes is an American Negro poet and has no choice but to be acutely aware of it. He is not the first American Negro to find the war between his social and artistic responsibilities all but irreconcilable.

> James Baldwin, "Sermons and Blues," *New York Times Book Review*, 29 March 1959, p. 6

WEBSTER SMALLEY   Hughes' point of view and purpose in his Harlem folk plays is summed up in his description of the final play in this collection:

> *Tambourines to Glory* is a fable, a folk ballad in stage form, told in broad and very simple terms—if you will, a comic strip, a

cartoon—about problems which can only convincingly be reduced to a comic strip if presented very cleanly, clearly, sharply, precisely, and with humor.

Hughes has done just this in all three plays ⟨*Little Ham, Simply Heavenly,* and *Tambourines to Glory*⟩. Technically, each is a comedy, but, however tongue-in-cheek his approach in *Tambourines to Glory,* Hughes has made the problem of good and evil central to the action. Thus, it is at once the most serious and the most dramatic of his comedies. Neither Ham ⟨in *Little Ham*⟩ nor Simple ⟨in *Simply Heavenly*⟩ ever comes to grips with a moral issue. Part of Ham's charm is that he is unaware that moral issues exist. Simple knows right from wrong, but there are so very many pleasant little sins lying in wait for him that we hardly blame him for straying, especially since he is such a gregarious being and his intended wife-to-be goes to bed so early.

Essie and Laura, in *Tambourines to Glory,* are presented as simply and forthrightly as are Ham and Simple, but there is no similarity of character. Essie and Laura are both strong individuals—Essie, in her goodness, and Laura, in her predilection toward chicanery. Symbolically, they represent two very real aspects of all revivalist, perhaps all religious, movements. The saint and the charlatan often live side by side, even in established religions, and sometimes exist in a single personality. Hughes chose to write a rousing musical melodrama about some aspects of Harlem religion. The result is a skillfully created, well-integrated musical play, written with humor, insight, and compassion.

It is the latter quality—Hughes' compassionate understanding of all his characters—that oftentimes minimizes dramatic action and conflict in his plays. Perhaps he likes his sinners too well, for he is inclined to justify their evil by mitigating circumstances. But it may be that he has never forgotten an early experience, gained shortly after his grandmother's death. He lived for a time in Kansas with a couple named Reed. Hughes has written that "Auntie Reed" was a devout Christian but "Uncle Reed" was a sinner, and has said, "No doubt from them I learned to like both Christians and sinners equally well." There can be no doubt that Hughes prefers the healthy sinner to the pretentious fake.

Villains are not plentiful in Hughes' Harlem plays. Big-Eyed Buddy Lomax (who informs us that he is really the Devil) is unique. Even he is a threat only through Laura's weakness for him (and all he represents). Hughes is

not as interested in a conventional conflict between protagonist and antago-
nist as in revealing the cracks in the self-protecting façades humans erect
to conceal their weaknesses. His characters are never merely subservient to
plot. Thus, even within the confines of melodrama, he is able to write a
moving and honest play.

> Webster Smalley, "Introduction," *Five Plays* by Langston Hughes (Bloomington:
> Indiana University Press, 1963), pp. xv–xvi

JAMES A. EMANUEL   "My soul has grown deep like the rivers,"
declares Hughes in one of his earliest and most famous poems, "The Negro
Speaks of Rivers." Negro soul is not a subject, but a complex of feelings
("*Yo no estudio al negro. Lo seinto,*" the author told Nicolás Guillén on his
second trip to Cuba in 1930). In Kansas City at the age of nine, on Independence Avenue and on Twelfth Street, Hughes was first impressed—outside
family circles—by the sound of the Negro soul: He heard the blues, his first
inspiration to write poetry.

He undertook a difficult task when he sought to communicate the poetry
of the blues through written words alone—and at a time when Bessie and
Clara Smith, and Ethel Waters, were popularizing the blues with all the
advantages that musical, vocal, and gestic art combine. While singing the
blues, these artists, with a stiffening of the back, could suggest historical
chain-gang chants to the spell-bound listener; with diverting wrist, torso,
or hip movements, they could lessen the potential monotony of the repeated
lines; with various facial expressions, they could signal the recall of much
of the spiritual beauty, or anguish, of Negro history. But the rigid blues
pattern, within which vocal artists and instrumentalists were free to evoke
and personalize an entire tradition, was a limitation to the poet. To give
artistic expression of permanent value to a form demanding simple diction,
repetition, and an elementary rhyme scheme raised problems. Examination
of a few of his best blues poems shows Hughes's contribution of a new verse
form to our literature.

Although the prize-winning title poem of *The Weary Blues* contains part
of a blues song "coming from a black man's soul," two-thirds of the lines
describe the piano player. The picture is vivid, but it is not a poetic transcrip-
tion of the blues form. In 1921 Hughes mailed to *The Crisis* a striking poem

closer to the required form, "Song for a Banjo Dance," which opens as follows:

> Shake your brown feet, honey,
> Shake your brown feet, chile,
> Shake your brown feet, honey,
> Shake 'em swift and wil'—
>   Get way back, honey,
>   Walk on over, darling,
>   Now! Come out
>   With your left.

In the prefatory pages of *Fine Clothes to the Jew*, Hughes explains: "The *Blues* . . . have a strict rhyme pattern: one long line repeated and a third line to rhyme with the first two. Sometimes the second line . . . is slightly changed and sometimes . . . it is omitted." This poem does not adhere to that pattern. Nor does it as a whole display enough of the traditional mood, which, the author's note goes on to say, "is almost always despondency, but when they are sung people laugh." Although not blues, this poem reflects the Negro soul through its spreading joy, its defiant rhyme that shakes itself at hovering melancholy.

James A. Emanuel, *Langston Hughes* (Boston: Twayne, 1967), pp. 137–38

LAURENCE LIEBERMAN   Langston Hughes's new poems, written shortly before his death last summer, catch fire from the Negro American's changing face. To a degree I would never have expected from his earlier work, his sensibility has kept pace with the times, and the intensity of his new concerns—helping him to shake loose old crippling mannerisms, the trade marks of his art—comes to fruition in many of the best poems of his career: "Northern Liberal," "Dinner Guest: Me," "Crowns and Garlands," to name a few.

Regrettably, in different poems, he is fatally prone to sympathize with starkly antithetical politics of race. A reader can appreciate his catholicity, his tolerance of the rival—and mutually hostile—views of his outspoken compatriots, from Martin Luther King to Stokely Carmichael, but we are tempted to ask, what are Hughes's politics? And if he has none, why not? The age demands intellectual commitment from its spokesmen. A poetry whose chief claim on our attention is moral, rather than aesthetic, must take sides politically. His impartiality is supportable in "Black Panther," a central thematic poem of "The Panther and the Lash." The panther, a symbol of the New Negro militancy, dramatizes the shift in politics from non-violence to Black Power, from a defensive to an offensive stance: Hughes stresses the essential underlying will to survival—against brutal odds—of either position. He is less concerned with approving or disapproving of Black Power than with demonstrating the necessity and inevitability of the shift, in today's racial crisis.

"Justice," an early poem that teaches the aesthetic value of rage, exhibits Hughes's knack for investing metaphor with a fierce potency that is as satisfying poetically as it is politically tumultuous:

> That justice is a blind goddess
> Is a thing to which we black are wise:
> Her bandage hides two festering sores
> That once perhaps were eyes.

But this skill is all but asphyxiated in many of the new poems by an ungovernable weakness for essayistic polemicizing that distracts the poet from the more serious demands of his art, and frequently undermines his poetics. Another technique that Hughes often employs successfully in the new poems is the chanting of names of key figures in the Negro Revolution. This primitive device has often been employed as a staple ingredient in good political poetry, as in Yeats's "Easter 1916." But when the poem relies too exclusively on this heroic cataloguing—whether of persons or events—for its structural mainstay, as in "Final Call," it sinks under the freight of self-conscious historicity.

> Laurence Leiberman, "Poetry and Chronicle," *Poetry* 112, No. 5 (August 1968): 339–40

WILLIAM MILES   Few writers have been as prolific in their attempt to describe and interpret Negro American life as Langston Hughes. Poet, novelist, short story writer, and dramatist, "he writes to express those truths he feels need expressing about characters he believes need to be recognized" ⟨Webster Smalley⟩. One such truth is the forced isolation of the majority of black people by the culture within which they are forced by circumstance to exist. The intensity and repressiveness of such isolation alienates the black person not only from the culture at large, but frequently from his own brothers as well. This is the theme of Hughes' powerful one-act play, *Soul Gone Home*. In less than four pages of text he presents a tragic and poignant picture of a people so isolated from each other that the establishment of meaningful emotional relationship is no longer possible.

The theme of isolation is not, of course, original with Hughes. What is original in *Soul Gone Home*, however, is the manner in which this theme is treated. The play is a fantasy of both situation and structure. Reality as we commonly experience it is replaced by the unreal, the dreamlike; the usual physical laws governing life and death are suspended. Yet the emphasis of the play is clearly on things as they exist in actuality. The play is about a situation resulting from the condition of black people in America. The immediate situation explored within the fantastic world of the play is itself unreal: a conflict between an uncaring mother and the ghost of her dead son in which the latter condemns his mother ("You been a hell of a mamma! . . . I say you been a no-good mamma.") because she failed to provide him with the necessities of life, food, clothing, "manners and morals."

This internal conflict in the realm of fantasy forms the center of the drama, but the structural limits are defined by reality. *Soul Gone Home* begins with the mother grieving over her son's body and concludes with his removal by the ambulance drivers. However, Hughes has constructed even these apparently real incidents in such a way as to render them unreal. For example, the opening stage direction informs us that the mother is "loudly simulating grief" and the play ends on the same note with her again feigning grief in the presence of the indifferent ambulance drivers.

The importance of both this underlying structure and the unreality of the situation is that they immediately establish the fact of the isolated condition of the mother and son. The boy is, of course, apart from the real world in the sense that he is dead, and, likewise, the mother is removed by the very fact that she can openly converse with him. Indeed, the mother is actually doubly removed: her "real" life, or what glimpses we get of it, is characterized by a sense of unreality. Symbolically, therefore, she is not a part of the reality defined by the general society, and her being outside in large part is the result of her race. To emphasize this fact, Hughes underlines the isolated condition of both mother and son through their lack of relatedness to the white ambulance drivers. Both are completely oblivious and indifferent to the dead boy and the tears of the "grieving" mother, and their lack of responsiveness to the situation is a measure of the vast gulf separating black and white.

Structurally, therefore, fantasy functions to establish the complete physical isolation of the two main characters from the real world. The focal point
of the play, the inability of mother and son to relate on the emotional level,
exists in a cause-and-effect relationship with their isolation from the society:
forced and repressive physical isolation of one group by another results in
severe emotional alienation among members of the persecuted group. In
developing and emphasizing this emotional element, Hughes superimposes
upon his fantasy clear implications of stark reality. Thus the total effect of
Soul Gone Home is realism, and while the central conflict may be internal,
the implied commentary relates wholly to the external world. ⟨. . .⟩

Through the skillful combination of situation, structure, character and
symbol, Hughes has produced a compact and powerful play of a people so
isolated that even the ordinarily secure relationship between mother and
son is impossible. And while this thematic consideration is immediately
revelant to the Negro American, *Soul Gone Home* does achieve a sense of
universality in that its social commentary relates to any oppressed minority.

> William Miles, "Isolation in Langston Hughes' *Soul Gone Home*," *Five Black Writers:
> Essays on Wright, Ellison, Baldwin, Hughes, and Leroi Jones,* ed. Donald B. Gibson
> (New York: New York University Press, 1970), pp. 178–79, 182

FAITH BERRY   The House Un-American Activities Committee
(HUAC) was reaching out like an octopus and, by 1950, was referring to
Hughes in its documents. ⟨. . .⟩

Hughes did not know what the repercussions would be when he appeared
before the McCarthy Committee on March 26, 1953. He did know that
some witnesses, in order to save themselves, had destroyed others by "naming
names," which he was determined not to do. He knew, too, that others
who had taken the Fifth Amendment had ended up in jail or, worse, as
suicides. Having seen enough careers broken, he could not be sure that the
same would not happen to him. ⟨. . .⟩

When McCarthy sounded the gavel at the public hearing and came face
to face with Hughes and his lawyer for this encounter, Frank D. Reeves, it
appeared they were meeting for the first time. In fact, they had already met
privately in executive session—first with ⟨Roy⟩ Cohn and ⟨G. David⟩ Schine,
and then in the Senator's office. Cohn, a harsher interrogator than Schine,
had grilled Hughes about some of his writings. McCarthy, however, was

anxious that a renowned American author should not become a "hostile witness." He had worked out an arrangement whereby Hughes would not be asked to "name names" of known Communists, but only in order to admit tacitly his own pro-Communist sympathies and writings. Having been indecisive about whether he would testify at all, after much private discussion with Reeves, he finally agreed to cooperate in the McCarthy scenario. He feared the worst if he didn't. Raising his right hand, he said, "I do," when the Senator asked him, "Do you swear to tell the whole truth and nothing but the truth, so help you God?"

On the witness stand, Hughes confessed that "there was such a period" when Cohn asked whether he had been a believer in the Soviet form of government; and "I certainly did," when questioned whether he wrote poetry which reflected his feelings during that time; and "That is correct, sir," when Cohn added, "I understand your testimony to be that you never actually joined the Communist Party." But so hard did he try to tell the truth about his past Soviet sympathies and at the same time sound like a patriotic American that he was only a shadow of himself. "A complete reorientation of my thinking and feelings occurred roughly four or five years ago," he offered, but Cohn quickly interjected "I notice that in 1949 you made a statement in defense of the Communist leaders who were on trial, which was in the *Daily Worker*." Hughes said he believed "one can and does" get a fair trial in America. Pressed to defend "When a Man Sees Red" and other works, he got away with, "They do not represent my current thinking," and "I have more recent books I would prefer." Asked to explain his "complete change in ideology," he affirmed, "I have always been a believer in the American form of government." There were moments when, pulverized into submission, he did disparage the Soviet Union. Praised by Southern Senator John McClellan for his "refreshing and comforting testimony," Hughes finally asked McCarthy, after about an hour of the inquisition, "Am I excused now, sir?" McCarthy finally let him go, after announcing he had "included in the record, on request," Hughes's earlier poem, "Goodbye, Christ" "to show the type of thinking of Mr. Hughes at that time." To show he also had been a "friendly witness," he sought assurance from the poet that he had not been "in any way mistreated by the staff or by the Committee." The capitulation was complete, from beginning to end.

Faith Berry, *Langston Hughes: Before and Beyond Harlem* (Westport, CT: Lawrence Hill, 1983), pp. 317–19

DAVID NICHOLSON   In forging his individual style, Hughes broke with the genteel tradition of Afro-American letters. His contemporary Countee Cullen used elevated forms such as the sonnet for his similarly elevated subject matter; Hughes early wrote in free verse, perhaps helped, ⟨Arnold⟩ Rampersad speculates, by the examples of Walt Whitman and Carl Sandburg. He soon came to use black common speech and to write of ordinary people—his *Fine Clothes to the Jew*, which Rampersad calls Hughes' "most brilliant book of poems, and one of the more astonishing books of verse ever published in the United States," was soundly criticized, not because of its title, but because many found his portraits of gamblers, musicians and prostitutes offensive. Though Hughes occasionally wrote in dialect that aped the work of Paul Laurence Dunbar, his mature style was simple and elegant, framed with the rhythm, tone and color of the blues. And, unlike Dunbar, he never felt that in using the vernacular he had betrayed his talents.

In this regard—creating art that in content and form fall "deliberately within the range of authentic blues emotion and blues culture"—Hughes proves an important international influence. Nicolás Guillén, the national poet of Cuba, began on Hughes' advice to use the rhythms of the drum-based, call-and-response *son* in his work; Léopold Sédar Senghor and Léon Damas would cite him as essential to their development of the French African and Caribbean literary movement-cum-philosophy known as *Négritude*. ⟨. . .⟩

If Hughes was "anxious for love and a settled identity," he found it in his relationship with his black audience. He wanted, he wrote in his journals, "To create a Negro culture in America—a real, solid, sane racial something growing out of the folk life, not copied from another, even though surrounding race." In his elevation of black folk forms, he succeeded as well or better than his comtemporaries or any of those who have come after him.

David Nicholson, "Langston Hughes: Lives of the Poet" [review of *The Life of Langston Hughes*, Vol. 1, by Arnold Rampersad], *Washington Post Book World*, 4 January 1987, p. 2

ARNOLD RAMPERSAD   Between Hughes, on the one hand, and ⟨James⟩ Baldwin and ⟨Ralph⟩ Ellison, on the other, was one difference far greater than any between the latter writers. While Langston psychologically needed the race in order to survive and flourish, their deepest needs as artists and human beings were evidently elsewhere. He wanted young black writers to be objective about the race, but not to scorn or to flee it. And all around him he saw young blacks confused by the rhetoric of integration and preparing to flee the race even when they made excoriating cries as exquisitely as Baldwin did in his essays. Baldwin's second novel had contained no black characters; his third would include blacks, but as characters secondary to his hero, a white American writer. To some extent, Baldwin was much more concerned with the mighty and dangerous challenge of illuminating—as a virtual pioneer in modern American fiction—the homosexual condition than with the challenge of writing about race, which by contrast had been exhaustively treated.

Although Langston did not dispute the right of black authors to tell any story they chose, a black writer's place was at home, which in Manhattan was Harlem—a perfectly fine place if not deserted by its human talent. At the end of ⟨. . .⟩ 1960, when he spoke on the WABC television program "Expedition: New York," he stressed the positive. Harlem a congested area? "It is. Congested with people. All kinds. And I'm lucky enough to call a great many of them my friends." This cheerful, uncritical acceptance of Harlem was anathema to the tortured James Baldwin, whose "Fifth Avenue Uptown," his portrait of the Harlem community in *Esquire* magazine the previous July, had showed warts and only warts: poverty, degradation, filth, and "the silent, accumulating contempt and hatred of a people."

In the half-decade of integration since 1954, and despite stirring essays on race by Baldwin and other blacks, Langston was one of the few black writers of any consequence to champion racial consciousness as a source of inspiration for black artists. No such call came from Richard Wright, Gwendolyn Brooks, Melvin Tolson, Robert Hayden, Ralph Ellison, Chester Himes, or—to be sure—Frank Yerby, by far the most financially successful Afro-American author, as a writer of avidly read Southern romances. And, as the youngest writers began slowly to perceive an emptiness in their art and lives in spite of the afflated rhetoric of integration, they would turn to Hughes more than to any other living author. "Oh if the nurse would let me travel through Harlem with you as the guide," Conrad Kent Rivers wrote to him, "I, too, could sing of black America." "The Negro Speaks of Rivers," Rivers admitted, "changed my outlook toward myself as a Negro." Lorraine Hansberry, writing to Langston to dissociate herself from an *Esquire* attack on him by Baldwin which she allegedly had sanctioned, confirmed her regard for him "not only as my mentor but the poet laureate of our people." (As for Baldwin's attack on Langston, she told a journalist, "Jimmy shows Langston no *respect.* . . . He refers to Langston in public the way we niggers usually talk in private to each other.")

Arnold Rampersad, *The Life of Langston Hughes* (New York: Oxford University Press, 1988), Vol. 2, pp. 297–98

R. BAXTER MILLER   Though Hughes accepted explicitly the Marxist belief that history produces events and men—namely, the doctrine of Darwinian determinism—he believed as well that people determine their own fate, for he almost never minimized human will. When fiscal policies brought on the Great Depression of the United States in the 1930s and the subsequent aggression helped provoke World War II, he still dreamed.

Hughes, believing in Marxism more discursively than naturally, is ambiguous on the subject. Facing the basic conceptions of materialism and colonialism, he seeks to bridge the rupture between the material form of the English language and the ironic need to materialize through this very language those ideas that seem at odds with a Euro-American perspective. To him, writing becomes intellectual armament against colonialism throughout the world. While *A New Song* (1938) illustrates his inability at the age of thirty-six to analyze the complex flaws of liberal idealism, he is not naive about historical evil.

Hughes resists the Marxist tendency to repress conscience in order to make history evolve according to some preordained pattern. *Jim Crow's Last Stand* (1943) shows his intransigence to disillusion and his potential for self-recovery.

> Some folks think
> By burning books
> They burn freedom.
> . . . .
> Some folks think
> By lynching a Negro
> They lynch freedom.
> But freedom
> Stands up and laughs
> In their faces,
> And says,
> You'll *never kill me!* ["Freedom"]

Even in *Good Morning Revolution*, which lacks the structural and chronologi-cal unity of the other published works, the tension appears strongly. And when Hughes subsequently confronts the social history of the years 1963–67, including the deaths of martyrs, and seems sometimes to abandon all hope, it is rarely for long. Where such psychological complexities recur in *Ask Your Mama* (1961), memory and human consciousness take shape through words. Hughes provides, finally, not the mere reflection of history but a brilliant and metaphoric code by which to read the record profoundly. The narrative conscience does threaten in *The Panther and the Lash* (1967) to regress into inevitable brutality, as the counterpart to an even greater sav-agery imposed upon the Black self ⟨. . .⟩ Yet, the collapse remains incomplete.

Langston Hughes gives verbal shape to the political and psychological struggle of humanity, particularly in American civilization. What is necessary for a reassessment of his political imagination is a careful reading of the developmental cycle that passes from direct didacticism (*A New Song*, 1938) through a more liberal and lyrical kind of political statement (*Jim Crow's Last Stand*, 1943) to a more symbolic rendition of the political world (*Good Morning Revolution*, 1925–53, collected 1972) and finally to a great psycho-logical complexity (*Ask Your Mama*, 1961). Near the end of Hughes' life (*The Panther and the Lash*, 1967) his political imagination returns almost to the tone with which it began, though with some lyrical qualification.

R. Baxter Miller, *The Art and Imagination of Langston Hughes* (Lexington: University Press of Kentucky, 1989), pp. 67–69

ALICE WALKER   When I started thinking about this piece on Langston I was surprised to find his presence so much further away than I imagined it ever could be. For Langston's spirit is one that stayed around, after his death, for many of us. Five years after he died I could still "feel" him, as if he were sitting in my living room or at the top of a tree in my yard. Even now, every once in a while, he floats quite vividly through my dreams, teaching me as a spirit in much the same way he did as a person. What, I sometimes wonder, does this mean?

I think it means that some of us, as we grow and suffer and struggle and age—turn into love. We may continue to be our ordinary selves, but in fact, a transformation occurs. I suspect we let go of everything that does not matter, even our own names, sometimes, so that when a bright hopeful face of anything greets us, we are ready to bestow a smile. The radiance of which lasts an entire life.

By the time I met him, Langston Hughes had turned into love. That is what I met. That is what continues to comfort me through various nights. That is what continues to be a sun. This is true, I believe, for many people.

And now the only question is: How can we honor this?

I think we can honor Langston's memory by remembering that in this life, the Christian church notwithstanding, we are not really required to attain perfection, which is impossible, but to learn to love, which is.

This is almost as hard as attaining perfection, but that is only because we are afraid. I like to think of something Mahatma Gandhi did, in pondering our situation. There was a Hindu man who had killed a Moslem child, and he came to Gandhi in his grief and asked what he could do to atone. Gandhi said: adopt a Moslem child, and raise him as a Moslem. This is a brilliant response, and becomes more profound the longer one studies it.

In this context, I think of a line in Langston's autobiography where he dismisses Zora Neale Hurston with the line: "Girls are funny creatures." I am thankful that twenty-five years after writing that line Langston, on meeting me, showed no trace of thinking "Girls are funny creatures," but rather responded to me as if I were his own child, my future as a person and a writer his own concern.

Alice Walker, "Turning into Love: Some Thoughts on Surviving and Meeting Langston Hughes," *Callaloo* 12, No. 4 (Fall 1989): 665

RICHARD NELSON   In 1922, Hughes wrote a poem called "Mulatto," but he did not pursue that theme of legitimacy again until 1931, when he confronted the issue in a play by the same name. *Mulatto* was not performed until 1935, when it opened on Broadway to hostile reviews.

Set in Georgia, the play, like the original poem, was an effort to confront the tragedy of interracial hatred as a form of family destruction. Hughes linked class oppression to racism in the play, as a small-time country politician, Fred Higgins, wishes "the South had more men like Bilbo and Rankin." But Hughes's central theme was the moral corrosiveness of racial exploitation. Higgins chastises Colonel Norwood, the white father of four unacknowledged Mulatto children:

> Nothing but blacks in the house—a man gets soft like niggers are
> inside. (*Puffing at cigar*). And living with a colored woman! Of
> course, I know we all have 'em. I didn't know you could make use
> of a white girl till I was past twenty. Thought too much o' white
> women for that—but I've given many a yellow gal a baby in my
> time (*Long puff at cigar*). But for a man's house you need a wife
> not a black woman.

Colonel Norwood is killed by his son as a tragic consequence of failing
to acknowledge their true relation, despite being bound by it. Bert, the son,
is pursued by a mob of angry whites, and kills himself to avoid being lynched.
Before his death, his mother and Norwood's unacknowledged mate, Cora,
berates the father's corpse: "Col. Tom, you hear me? Our boy out there
runnin'. (*Fiercely*) You said he was ma boy—*ma* bastard boy. I heard you
. . . but he's yours too . . . but yonder in de dark runnin'—from you' people,
from white People." In failing to recognize his common humanity with his
mate and son, Norwood brings tragedy and forfeits his own legitimacy as a
father. Hughes could offer no resolution but death for the abandoned son
and madness for his twice-abandoned mother. But there is no effort to
preserve paternal or white authority in the play's conclusion.

Richard Nelson, "Ironic Inversions: Pastoralism in C. Vann Woodward and Langston
Hughes," *Aesthetic Frontiers: The Machiavellian Tradition and the Southern Imagination*
(Jackson: University of Mississippi Press, 1990), pp. 180–81

KAREN JACKSON FORD   ⟨. . .⟩ "The Negro Speaks of Rivers"
is one of Hughes's most uncharacteristic poems, and yet it has defined his
reputation, along with a small but constant selection of other poems included
in anthologies. "The Negro Speaks of Rivers," "A House in Taos," "The
Weary Blues," "Montage of a Dream Deferred," "Theme for English B,"
"Refugee in America," and "I, Too"—these poems invariably comprise his
anthology repertoire despite the fact that none of them typifies his writing.
What makes these poems atypical is exactly what makes them appealing
and intelligible to the scholars who edit anthologies—their complexity.
True, anthologies produced in the current market, which is hospitable to
the African-American tradition and to canon reform, now include a brief
selection of poems in black folk forms. But even though Hughes has fared
better in anthologies than most African-American writers, only a small and

predictable segment of his poetry has been preserved. A look back through the original volumes of poetry, and even through the severely redrawn *Selected Poems*, reveals a wealth of simpler poems we ought to be reading. ⟨. . .⟩

The repression of the great bulk of Hughes's poems is the result of chronic critical scorn for their simplicity. Throughout his long career, but especially after his first two volumes of poetry (readers were at first willing to assume that a youthful poet might grow to be more complex), his books received their harshest reviews for a variety of "flaws" that all originate in an aesthetics of simplicity. From his first book, *The Weary Blues* (1926), to his last one, *The Panther and the Lash* (1967), the reviews invoke a litany of faults: the poems are superficial, infantile, silly, small, unpoetic, common, jejune, iterative, and, of course, simple. Even his admirers reluctantly conclude that Hughes's poetics failed. Saunders Redding flatly opposes simplicity and artfulness: "While Hughes's rejection of his own growth shows an admirable loyalty to his self-commitment as the poet of the 'simple, Negro commonfolk' . . . it does a disservice to his art." James Baldwin, who recognizes the potential of simplicity as an artistic principle, faults the poems for "tak[ing] refuge . . . in a fake simplicity in order to avoid the very difficult simplicity of the experience."

Despite a lifetime of critical disappointments, then, Hughes remained loyal to the aesthetic program he had outlined in 1926 in his decisive poetic treatise, "The Negro Artist and the Racial Mountain." There he had predicted that the common people would "give to this world its truly great Negro artist, the one who is not afraid to be himself," a poet who would explore the "great field of unused [folk] material ready for his art" and recognize that this source would provide "sufficient matter to furnish a black artist with a lifetime of creative work." This is clearly a portrait of the poet Hughes would become, and he maintained his fidelity to this ideal at great cost to his literary reputation.

Karen Jackson Ford, "Do Right to Write Right: Langston Hughes's Aesthetics of Simplicity," *Twentieth Century Literature* 38, No. 4 (Winter 1992): 436–38

⬖ *Bibliography*

The Weary Blues. 1926.

Fine Clothes to the Jew. 1927.

Not without Laughter. 1930.

The Negro Mother and Other Dramatic Recitations. 1931.

Dear Lovely Death. 1931.

The Dream Keeper and Other Poems. 1932.

Popo and Fifina, Children of Haiti (with Arna Bontemps). 1932.

Scottsboro Limited: Four Poems and a Play in Verse. 1932.

The Ways of White Folks. 1934.

A New Song. 1938.

The Big Sea: An Autobiography. 1940.

Shakespeare in Harlem. 1942.

Freedom's Plow. 1943.

Jim Crow's Last Stand. 1943.

Lament for Dark Peoples and Other Poems. Ed. H. Driessen. 1944.

This Is My Land (with Toy Harper and La Villa Tullos). c. 1945.

Fields of Wonder. 1947.

Street Scene (adapter; with Kurt Weill). 1948.

Cuba Libre: Poems by Nicolás Guillén (translator; with Ben Frederic Carruthers). 1948.

Troubled Island (adapter; with William Grant Still). 1949.

One-Way Ticket. 1949.

The Poetry of the Negro 1746–1949 (editor; with Arna Bontemps). 1949, 1970.

Simple Speaks His Mind. 1950.

Montage of a Dream Deferred. 1951.

The First Book of Negroes. 1952.

Laughing to Keep from Crying. 1952.

Simple Takes a Wife. 1953.

Famous American Negroes. 1954.

The First Book of Rhythms. 1954.

Famous Negro Music Makers. 1955.

The First Book of Jazz. 1955.

The Sweet Flypaper of Life (with Roy De Carava). 1955.

The First Book of the West Indies. 1956.

I Wonder as I Wander: An Autobiographical Journey. 1956.

A Pictorial History of the Negro in America (with Milton Meltzer). 1956, 1963, 1968.

Selected Poems of Gabriela Mistral (translator). 1957.

Simple Stakes a Claim. 1957.

The Book of Negro Folklore (editor; with Arna Bontemps). 1958.

Famous Negro Heroes of America. 1958.

The Langston Hughes Reader. 1958.

Tambourines to Glory. 1958.

Simply Heavenly: A Comedy with Music (with David Martin). 1959.

Selected Poems. 1959.

An African Treasury (editor). 1960.

The First Book of Africa. 1960, 1964.

Ask Your Mama: Twelve Moods for Jazz. 1961.

The Best of Simple. 1961.

Fight for Freedom: The Story of NAACP. 1962.

Five Plays. Ed. Webster Smalley. 1963.

Poems from Black Africa (editor). 1963.

Something in Common and Other Stories. 1963.

New Negro Poets U.S.A. (editor). 1964.

Simple's Uncle Sam. 1965.

The Book of Negro Humor (editor). 1965.

The Best Short Stories by Negro Writers: Anthology from 1899 to the Present (editor). 1967.

Black Magic: A Pictorial History of the Negro in American Entertainment (with Milton Meltzer). 1967.

The Panther and the Lash: Poems of Our Times. 1967.

Black Misery. 1969.

Don't You Turn Back: Poems. Ed. Lee Bennett Hopkins. 1969.

Good Morning, Revolution: Uncollected Social Protest Writings. Ed. Faith Berry. 1973.

Langston Hughes in the Hispanic World and Haiti. Ed. Edward J. Mullen. 1977.

Arna Bontemps–Langston Hughes Letters 1925–1967. Ed. Charles H. Nichols. 1980.

Mule Bone: A Comedy of Negro Life (with Zora Neale Hurston). Ed. George Houston Bass and Henry Louis Gates, Jr. 1991.

Georgia Douglas Johnson
1886–1966

GEORGIA DOUGLAS CAMP JOHNSON was born on September 10, 1886, to George and Laura Jackson Camp in Atlanta, Georgia. Johnson attended public schools in Atlanta and went on to Atlanta University. She later attended Howard University in Washington, D.C., and the Oberlin Conservatory of Music in Ohio. She married Henry Lincoln Johnson in 1903. They had two sons, Henry Lincoln, Jr., and Peter Douglas.

Johnson was capable of great periods of creativity, and her interests were as varied as her efforts were concentrated. As early as 1905 her poetry appeared in the *Voice of the Negro* and later in the *Crisis* and other periodicals. Her first book, *The Heart of a Woman*, did not appear until 1918. She was characterized by critics as a black feminist poet, although her early poems do not focus on themes of race or politics. She was essentially of the genteel school and much overshadowed by Sara Teasdale. Her poems, like Teasdale's, are generally conventional in form, romantic in tone, and short in length.

Johnson's second volume of poetry, *Bronze*, was published in 1922. These poems are marked by a clear development of racial consciousness and a focus on black history. By the time *Bronze* was published, Johnson had fallen in with a circle of black notables, such as W. E. B. Du Bois, Countee Cullen, Sterling Brown, Benjamin Brawley, James Weldon Johnson, and others. This volume was more widely read and more favorably reviewed than her first. When Johnson's husband died in 1925, she took on greater financial responsibilities, but her literary career was not dramatically affected. Both of her sons were attending Dartmouth and her literary gatherings were still growing in number. In 1927 Johnson won the *Opportunity* prize for her one-act play *Plumes* and in the same year produced her drama *Blue Blood* in New York.

Johnson's third collection of poetry, *An Autumn Love Cycle*, was published in 1928. It represents something of a departure from *Bronze*. The author returns to her earlier themes of love and loss. During the depression, however, Johnson focused primarily on the writing of drama that addressed racial and gender concerns. Her play *Sunday Morning in the South* was written to show support for the antilynching campaign. *Blue-Eyed Black Boy* and *Safe* have similar themes of social protest and were submitted for production to the Federal Theatre Projected but rejected along with three of her other plays. *Sunday Morning in the South* was published posthumously in *Black Theatre, U.S.A.*, edited by James V. Hatch and Ted Shine (1974). Johnson also wrote two plays that tell of the struggles of escaping to freedom in the North, *Frederick Douglass* and *William and Ellen Craft*, both published in *Negro History in Thirteen Plays*, edited by Willis Richardson and May Miller (1935).

Although Johnson focused her efforts on drama at this time, her poetry continued to appear in various periodicals. She was also much involved with the social and political life of Washington. She held various government positions, including Commissioner of Conciliation for the Department of Labor from 1925 to 1934. Her final volume of poetry, *Share My World*, appeared in 1962. Atlanta University presented her with an honorary doctorate in literature in 1965. Georgia Douglas Johnson died on May 14, 1966.

◈ *Critical Extracts*

WILLIAM STANLEY BRAITHWAITE   The poems in this book are intensely feminine and for me this means more than anything else that they are deeply human. We are yet scarcely aware, in spite of our boasted twentieth-century progress, of what lies deeply hidden, of mystery and passion, of domestic love and joy and sorrow, of romantic visions and practical ambitions, in the heart of a woman. The emancipation of woman is yet to be wholly accomplished; though woman has stamped her image on every age of the world's history, and in the heart of almost every man since time began, it is only a little over half of a century since she has either spoken or acted with a sense of freedom. During this time she has made little more than a start to catch up with man in the wonderful things he has to his credit; and yet all that man has to his credit would scarcely have been achieved except for the devotion and love and inspiring comradeship of woman.

Here, then, is lifted the veil, in these poignant songs and lyrics. To look upon what is revealed is to give one a sense of infinite sympathy; to make one kneel in spirit to the marvelous patience, the wonderful endurance, the persistent faith, which are hidden in this nature.

> The heart of a woman falls back with the night,
> And enters some alien cage in its plight,
> And tries to forget it has dreamed of the stars
> While it breaks, breaks, breaks on the sheltering bars.

sings the poet. And

> The songs of the singer
>   Are tones that repeat
> The cry of the heart
>   Till it ceases to beat.

This verse just quoted is from "The Dreams of the Dreamer," and with the previous quotation tells us that this woman's heart is keyed in the plaintive, knows the sorrowful agents of life and experience which knock and enter at the door of dreams. But women have made the saddest songs of the world, Sappho no less than Elizabeth Barrett Browning, Ruth the Moabite no less than Amy Levy, the Jewess who broke her heart against the London pavements; and no less does sadness echo its tender and appealing sigh in these songs and lyrics of Georgia Douglas Johnson. But sadness is a kind of felicity with woman, paradoxical as it may seem; and it is so because through this inexplicable felicity *they* touched, intuitionally caress, reality.

So here engaging life at its most reserved sources, whether the form or substance through which it articulates be nature, or the seasons, touch of hands or lips, love, desire, or any of the emotional abstractions which sweep like fire or wind or cooling water through the blood, Mrs. Johnson creates just the reality of woman's heart and experience with astonishing raptures. It is a kind of privilege to know so much about the secrets of woman's nature, a privilege all the more to be cherished when given, as in these poems, with such exquisite utterance, with such a lyric sensibility.

William Stanley Braithwaite, "Introduction," *The Heart of a Woman and Other Poems* by Georgia Douglas Johnson (Boston: Cornhill Co., 1918), pp. vii–ix

---

J. R. FAUSET   In these days of *vers libre* and the deliberate straining for poetic effect these lyrics of Mrs. Johnson bring with them a certain sense of relief and freshness. Also the utter absence of the material theme makes appeal. We are all very wary of the war note and are glad to return to the softer pipings of old time themes—love, friendship, longing, despair—all of which are set forth in *The Heart of a Woman*.

The book has artistry, but it is its sincerity which gives it its value. Here are the little sharp experiences of life mirrored poignantly, sometimes feverishly, always truly. Each lyric is an instantaneous photograph of one of the many moments in existence which affect one briefly perhaps, but indelibly. Mr. Braithwaite says in his introduction that this author engages "life at its most reserved sources whether the form or substance through which it articulates be nature, or the seasons, touch of hands or lips, love, desire or any of the emotional abstractions which sweep like fire or wind or cooling water through the blood." The ability to give a faithful and recognizable portrayal of these sources, is Mrs. Johnson's distinction.

In this work, Mrs. Johnson, although a woman of color, is dealing with life as it is regardless of the part that she may play in the great drama. Here she is a woman of that imagination that characterizes any literary person choosing this field as a means of directing the thought of the world. Several of her poems bearing on the Negro race have appeared in the *Crisis*. In these efforts she manifests the radical tendencies characteristic of every thinking Negro of a developed mind and sings beautifully not in the tone of the lamentations of the prophets of old but, while portraying the trials and tribulations besetting a despised and rejected people, she sings the song of hope. In reading her works the inevitable impression is that it does not yet appear what she will be. Adhering to her task with the devotion hitherto manifested, there is no reason why she should not in the near future take rank among the best writers of the world.

J. R. Fauset, [Review of *The Heart of a Woman and Other Poems*], *Journal of Negro History* 4, No. 4 (October 1919): 467–68

W. E. B. DU BOIS   Those who know what it means to be a colored woman in 1922—and know it not so much in fact as in feeling, apprehension, unrest and delicate yet stern thought—must read Georgia Douglas Johnson's *Bronze*. Much of it will not touch this reader and that, and some of it will mystify and puzzle them as a sort of reiteration and over-emphasis. But none can fail to be caught here and there by a word—a phrase—a period that tells a life history or even paints the history of a generation. Can you not see that marching of the mantled with

> Voices strange to ecstasy?

Have you ever looked on the "twilight faces" of their throngs, or seen the black mother with her son when

> Her heart is sandaling his feet?

Or can you not conceive that infinite sorrow of a dark child wandering the world:

> Seeking the breast of an unknown face!

I hope Mrs. Johnson will have wide reading. Her word is simple, sometimes trite, but it is singularly sincere and true, and as a revelation of the soul struggle of the women of a race it is invaluable.

> W. E. B. Du Bois, "Foreword," *Bronze: A Book of Verse* by Georgia Douglas Johnson (Boston: B. J. Brimmer Co., 1922), p. 7

ALAIN LEROY LOCKE   In *Bronze*, Mrs. Johnson has at last come to her own—if not also in a peculiar way, *into* her own. A certain maturity that is to be expected of a third volume of verse, is here, but it is the homecoming of the mind and heart to intimately racial thought and experience which is to be especially noted and commended. We can say of this that it is timely both for the author and her readers: for her, it represents the fruition of a premeditated plan not to speak racially until she has learned to speak and attract attention in the universal key; for her readers, of many classes and sections of opinion, it represents more perhaps an occasion of seeing the "color problem" at the heart, as it affects the inner life. Even if it were not very readable poetry, it would, from this latter point of view, be important as human documentation of a much needed sort. "Not wholly this or that"—"Frail children of sorrow, determined by a hue"—"Shall I say, 'My son, you're branded in this country's pageantry' "—the phrase Du Bois has singled out, "With voices strange to ecstasy"—"This spirit-choking atmosphere"—"My every fibre fierce rebels, against this servile rôle"—or

> Don't knock at my door, little child
>   I cannot let you in;
> You know not what a world this is—

there are volumes in these phrases. After this, the race question becomes, as it must to all intelligent observers, a human problem, a common problem.

One of Mrs. Johnson's literary virtues is condensation. She often distills the trite and commonplace into an elixir. Following the old-fashioned lyric strain and the sentimentalist cult of the common emotions, she succeeds because by sincerity and condensation, her poetry escapes to a large extent its own limitations. Here in the subject of these verses, there is however a double pitfall; avoiding sentimentality is to come dangerously close to propaganda. This is also deftly avoided—more by instinct than by calculation. Mrs. Johnson's silences and periods are eloquent, she stops short of the preachy and prosaic and is always lyrical and human. Almost before one has shaped his life to "Oh! the pity of it", a certain fresh breeze of faith and courage blows over the heart, and the mind revives to a healthy, humanistic optimist. Mrs. Johnson seems to me to hear a message, a message that gains through being softly but intensely insinuated between the lines of her poems—"Let the traditional instincts of women heal the world that travails under the accumulated woes of the uncompensated instincts of men", or to speak more in her way, "May the saving grace of the mother-heart save humanity."

Alain Leroy Locke, [Review of *Bronze: A Book of Verse*], *Crisis* 25, No. 4 (February 1923): 161

EFFIE LEE NEWSOME   It is well-nigh impossible to think of this vital product from the pen of Georgia Douglas Johnson without having communicated to one some of the intense conviction that WROUGHT it into being. It has been stated that authors can convince only to the extent of their persuasion: Georgia Douglas Johnson has molded with the very pulsations of her heart.

Her heart—for this is the potent factor in her creative force—has molded a "Bronze" that challenges not altogether with the sharp angles of accusation, but as well with the graceliness of heart's call to heart for sympathy in the problems of race; as in "The Octoroon;" as also in the ever-recurring light and shadow theme of colored woman's motherhood:

The infant eyes look out amazed upon the frowning earth,
A stranger, in a land now strange, child of the mantled
    birth;
Waxing, he wonders more and more; the scowling grows
    apace,
A world, behind its barring doors, reviles his ebon face!

And we must quote, further, the two lines that conclude if not solve the problem of the poem:

Yet from this maelstrom issues forth a God-like entity,
That loves a world all loveless, and smiles on Calvary!

In ending this finesse of workmanship Mrs. Johnson—or still shall we say, "her heart?"—polishes the bronze with the glory and rich lustre that bronze alone can know. There are inspiring paeans at the end of the work:

Into the very star-shine, lo! they come
Wearing the bays of victory complete!

—to quote in connection with closing tributes to black achievers, the last two verses from the sonnet that opens this book, burnished, in spite of all, now here, now there, with a brave "Optimism" that can glow thus:

We man our parts within life's tragic play.

Effie Lee Newsome, [Review of *Bronze: A Book of Verse*], *Opportunity* 1, No. 12 (December 1923): 337

ALAIN LOCKE   Voicing ⟨the⟩ yearning of woman for candid self-expression, Mrs. Johnson invades the province where convention has been most tyrannous and inveterate,—the experiences of love. And here she succeeds where others have failed; for they in over-sophistication, in terror of platitudes and the commonplace, have stressed the bizarre, the exceptional, in one way or another have over-intellectualized their message and overleapt the common elemental experience they would nevertheless express. Mrs. Johnson, on the contrary, in a simple declarative style, engages with ingenuous directness the moods and emotions of her themes.

Through you I entered Heaven and Hell
Knew rapture and despair.

Here is the requisite touch, certainly for the experiences of the heart. Greater sophistication would spoil the message. Fortunately, to the gift of a lyric style, delicate touch, rhapsodic in tone, authentic in timbre, there has been added a temperamental endowment of ardent sincerity of emotion, ingenuous candor of expression, and, happiest of all for the particular task, a naïve and unsophisticated spirit.

By way of a substantive message, Mrs. Johnson's philosophy of life is simple, unpretentious, but wholesome and spiritually invigorating. On the one hand, she belongs with those who, under the leadership of Sara Teasdale, have been rediscovering the Sapphic cult of love as the ecstasy of life, that cult of enthusiasm which leaps over the dilemma of optimism and pessimism, and accepting the paradoxes, pulses in the immediacies of life and rejoices openly in the glory of experience. In a deeper and somewhat more individual message, upon which she only verges, and which we believe will later be her most mature and original contribution, Mrs. Johnson probes under the experiences of love to the underlying forces of natural instinct which so fatalistically control our lives. [Especially is this evident in her suggestion of the tragic poignancy of Motherhood, where the consummation of love seems also the expiation of passion, and where, between the antagonisms of the dual role of Mother and Lover, we may suspect the real dilemma of womanhood to lie.]

Whatever the philosophical yield, however, we are grateful for the prospect of such lyricism. Seeking a pure lyric gold, Mrs. Johnson has gone straight to the mine of the heart. She has dug patiently in the veins of her own subjective experience. What she has gleaned has been treasured for the joy of the search and for its own intrinsic worth, and not exploited for the values of show and applause. Above all, her material has been expressed with a candor that shows that she brings to the poetic field what it lacks most,—the gift of the elemental touch. Few will deny that, with all its other excellences, the poetry of the generation needs just this touch to make it more vitally human and more spontaneously effective.

Alain Locke, "Foreword," *An Autumn Love Cycle* by Georgia Douglas Johnson (New York: Harold Vinal, 1928), pp. xvii–xix

---

ANNE SPENCER   Within the last ten years, Georgia Douglas Johnson has, through her publishers, brought out three volumes of lyrics, most of which employ—next to food—the oldest theme in the world, and would exquisitely complement a musical setting, here, too, in this united estate of America, where it is decidedly against the law,—Dred Scott, Monroe Doctrine, or, maybe, some unwritten cartel of Marque and Reprisal,—for any person of color to write of love without hypothecating atavistic jungle tones: the rumble of tom-tom, voodoo ebo, fetish of sagebrush and high spliced palm tree—all the primal universal passions often solely associated with Africa,—

Pardon, I did intend writing about Mrs. Johnson's latest book, *An Autumn Love Cycle,* but any digression is logical in an atmosphere where even an offering on the shrine of Parnassus must meet the agony of challenge: Aha! It is white. . . . How important! Lo, it is black! Alas! But Life, the book of poetry, cannot relate itself to unrelated persons. Silk purses are no more made of sows' ears than of rayon. The artificial has nothing to offer but surfaces. In these poems the author has come to terms with life, signed the valiant compromise, the Medean alternative, delivering her awareness over to pain. Her sentience speeds to its martyrdom crying,

> Fire—tears—
> And the torture-chamber,
> With the last maddening turn of the screw—

As one who believes the admixture of what we call human nature to be changeless, I can recall no better for any seasonal lovers than this newest idealization of the emotions:

> Oh night of love, your groves of strange content
> Project a thralldom over coming days;
> Exalted, derelict, and blind I went
> Unmindfully along Life's misty ways.

If with us the practice of a book of verses underneath the bough, or, better still, before the fire, has grown into sneering disrepute, it threatens the obsequies of the finest art, the gentle art of love-making. Lovers are the only persons left to us of any elegance at all. The last of the aristocrats, the Great Lover moves among his menials with a soul all prinked out in plumes, knee-buckles, and *diamant* shoon. Whatever his age, his past experiences, or physical characteristics, the true lover becomes an abstract creature, as shriven and innocent as at the day of his birth—or death . . .

> Consider me a melody
> That serves its simple turn,
> Or but the residue of fire
> That settles in the urn . . .

You will know that such snatches of song are unfair to the singer, but this, and more, Mrs. Johnson has poignantly lineated and set down for whatever God blessed folk remain in this hard-boiled day.

Anne Spencer, [Review of *An Autumn Love Cycle*], *Crisis* 36, No. 3 (March 1929): 87

MARITA ODETTE BONNER   It will have to be the old figure, I guess. It will have to be the figure of fire.—Love is fire.—But surely it is a fire.—Love must be a fire, lit in the beginning to warm us, to light us, to circle us in completely from the iciness of the Struggle—during our Night-of-Passage. In Youth, love is a flame mad and consuming, licking out to eat up Ideas and Ideals, true and false alike.

In Autumn, love is a smoldering fire. A yellow flame burning thinly here, a blue flame pouring steadily there, a red glow everywhere underneath the coals. A red glow smoldering under the coals, that must soon be covered with ashes from the Night.

In Autumn—a smoldering fire. A fire smoldering with yellow and blue jets. Yellow jets. Reflections of other flames. Yellow jets:

> Oh night of love,
> Your rapt ecstatic hours were mine.

Blue, steady, and a red glow all through:—

> Would I might mend
> the fabric of my youth
> For I would go a further while with you
> And drain the cup of Joy.

It is all there. The ashes of experiences burnt through, scorched through and become New "Welt," "Illusion," "Parody," "Delusion,"—Steadily—

And all through the *Autumn Love Cycle* you feel there glows before you, a life that has leapt eagerly to embrace all living, all loving. There is no forced pretenses at flights of emotion here—no sycophant, sexual, blue wailings. ⟨. . .⟩

Truly it is a fire that has burned steadily, bravely, unflinchingly. Surely here is a life lived steadily, a life lived whole.

Sticklers with their noses lowered to root out flaws might fail to see the steadiness, the wholeness sometimes when everything seems to sink suddenly laden with the heavy ornateness of the good old language of the nineteenth century. But there will always be rooters for flaws and sticklers for words and seekers for form—divorced—from content. And there will always be content—Life and Love whether it marches proudly and aristocratically in flawless form—whether it labors and heaves under a tangle of rocks and weeds.

And the *Autumn Love Cycle* swings completely—swings fully—glows with a reality that burns off any slight dross, any shade of imperfection and makes you draw deep scorching breath and say,

> Is this what it is to be—
> if you are young.

—If you are old—and if you are old—I guess you know that the fire of love even burns ashes.

Marita Odette Bonner, [Review of *An Autumn Love Cycle*], *Opportunity* 7, No. 4 (April 1929): 130

BENJAMIN BRAWLEY   Georgia Douglas was a teacher in Atlanta before becoming, in 1903, the wife of Henry Lincoln Johnson, later recorder of deeds in the District of Columbia. She is the author of three small volumes, *The Heart of a Woman* (1918), *Bronze* (1922), and *An Autumn Love Cycle* (1928). While much of her work transcends the bounds of race, her second booklet was dominated by the striving of the Negro; and her sympathy may also be seen in such a later poem as "Old Black Men."

> They have dreamed as young men dream
>   Of glory, love and power;
> They have hoped as youth will hope
>   Of life's sun-minted hour.
> They have seen as others saw
>   Their bubbles burst in air,
> And they have learned to live it down
>   As though they did not care.

In her earlier work Mrs. Johnson cultivated especially the poignant, sharply chiselled lyric that became so popular with Sara Teasdale and some other writers a decade or two ago. Later, however, there came into her verse a deeper, a more mellow note, as in "I Closed My Shutters Fast Last Night."

> I closed my shutters fast last night,
>   Reluctantly and slow,

So pleading was the purple sky
With all the lights hung low;
I left my lagging heart outside
Within the dark alone,
I heard it singing through the gloom
A wordless, anguished tone.

Upon my sleepless couch I lay
Until the tranquil morn
Came through the silver silences
To bring my heart forlorn,
Restoring it with calm caress
Unto its sheltered bower,
While whispering, "Await, await
Your golden, perfect hour."

Benjamin Brawley, *The Negro Genius* (New York: Dodd, Mead, 1937), pp. 219–20

CEDRIC DOVER   Georgia Douglass ⟨sic⟩ Johnson's poems were published in the anthologies of the Renaissance, her books appeared in the decade that marked its beginning and end, and her home has always been a center for the writers and artists who gave it color and shape. She is definitely of it; but equally definitely not in it. Her first volume, *The Heart of a Woman* (1918), echoes Sara Teasdale and shows real sensibility, but contains no hint of the ferment which, a little later, inspired Claude McKay's moving sonnets of protest, his evocative explorations of the Harlem scene, and his exquisite lyrics of nostalgia. ⟨. . .⟩

Mrs. Johnson's second book, *Bronze* (1922), reflects these departures from the poesy of the comfortable villa in the manner indicated by its title. The subject is still the heart of a woman, but now it is the heart of a colored woman aware of her social problem and the potentiality of the so-called hybrid. Therefore, it is unfortunate that *An Autumn Love Cycle* (1928) failed to concentrate her awareness. Instead of enlarging the new vitality, it reverts to the personal notes of her first poems, though it adds the aching maturity of a sensitive woman in her forties. The poet is again overwhelmed by herself.

Soon after the *Cycle*, the Depression swept away the Golden Brown and everything else that was supposedly golden in the days of mad prosperity. It should, by all analogies, have swept Mrs. Johnson away too, but she survived by turning her attention to other forms of writing. They did not get published, but they kept the flame alive.

The War might easily have extinguished it, but Mrs. Johnson responded with revived vigor to the changing scene. She added her voice to the Negro struggle for a full share in the democracy that demanded Negro lives and labor. She gave herself unstintingly and, at the same time, poured out a stream of effective poems and fighting songs. Today she is a poet born again of suffering and the social Holy Ghost.

It is an exceptional record. All the more exceptional when we view the sad procession of middle-class poets silenced by inability to find some dynamic in a transitional society. Mrs. Johnson has been saved from this fate, I think, by the circumstance of being a Negro. It has prevented class limitations from enclosing, and finally stifling, her. It has roused her passionate belief in ultimate justice and the coming brotherhood of man. It has given her that extra something apparent in her great sincerity and appealing simplicity.

These are qualities that assure admiration, even from those who have gone beyond idealization to the real means, the critical disciplines and endeavors, by which ideals are realized. They would be quite striking in an adequate and long overdue sifting of her collected poems. Such a bouquet would certainly have the fragrance of a rich and mellow personality, near enough to less generously endowed folk to be typical of cultivated thought in a large part of the colored world.

Indeed, her affinities are as integral to the interest of her poems as the quietly sharp differences. We expect chords of conventional familiarity amongst the offerings of her womanly heart—and we find them in abundance, as in these lines:

> I want to die while you love me,
> While yet you hold me fair;
> While laughter lies upon my lips
> And lights are in my hair.

Cedric Dover, "The Importance of Georgia Douglass Johnson," *Crisis* 59, No. 10 (December 1952): 633–44

WINONA L. FLETCHER   Encouraged by expectations that the Federal Theatre would be a haven for fledgling playwrights, that experimental productions not likely to get produced elsewhere would be mounted, that plays of social protest would be judged on their merits, Georgia Douglas Johnson submitted at least five plays to the Federal Theatre Project between 1935 and 1939, the year the project closed. *None* were accepted for publication in any of the producing units of FTP. Three of the plays submitted are specifically on the theme of lynching and rape; two are historical sketches based on the desperation of slaves to escape from servitude to freedom. The lynch mob lurks ubiquitously in the minds of the author and the characters of both of these dramas. A brief analysis of the dramas and of the FTP playreaders' evaluations of them can lead to an understanding of why Mrs. Johnson, and black playwrights in general, failed in the American theatre of the thirties—and any time when their serious dramas expose the evils of a racist society.

In the one-act drama, *Blue-Eyed Black Boy*, Jack Walter, a 21-year-old black man on his way home from work, innocently brushes against a white woman, is charged with an attempted attack, arrested and jailed. He becomes the intended victim of a lynch mob. Jack's mother, hearing the mob moving toward the jail to get her son, in desperation, retrieves a small ring from a secret hiding place. She then sends the black doctor, who is soon to marry her daughter, in haste to the governor with a message from "Pauline who gave birth to a son 21 years ago." She adds with emphasis:

> Just give him the ring and say, Pauline sent this, she says they goin' to lynch her son born 21 years ago, mind you say twenty-one years ago—then say—listen close—look into his eyes and you'll save him.

The ring and the message are delivered, the governor remembers, the militia is called out, the lynching is stopped, and Jack is sent home safely to his mother.

Like many of the revolutionary dramas of the sixties that are reminiscent of the social protest plays of the thirties, *Blue-Eyed Black Boy* is a tightly structured drama with compressed action. The entire playing time of the script is less than twenty minutes. Johnson, having already exhibited technical aptitude of high quality in her writing, handles exposition well through inference and understatement, plants a note of suspense, and concentrates on protesting the social realism of black women and their mulatto sons. The dialogue distinguishes between the simple dialect of the uneducated, older characters and the more polished speech of the young, educated characters. The audience never sees the blue-eyed boy and, while this contributes to the suspense, the omission might have contributed to the play being attacked as an "incomplete drama." ⟨. . .⟩

The action of *A Sunday Morning in the South* takes place in 1924 in a humble cottage occupied by a grandmother, Sue Jones, and her two young grandsons, Tom (19) and Bossie (7). Church music is heard from nearby as a neighbor, on her way to morning services, reports that a white woman has claimed "rape by a young black man." They all suspect that the rape charge is untrue but know it will fan more racial hatred and shudder at the thought of what will happen if the young man is found. Almost immediately, two white officers come with the girl who vaguely identifies Tom as the man who raped her. Despite the grandmother's pleas and assurance that Tom was at home asleep all night, the 19-year-old boy is arrested and supposedly taken to jail. Sue (in the second version) sends for help from "Miss Vilet, the good white woman," but learns that Tom is lynched before anybody can save him. The shock of the news kills Sue as the curtain falls.

Of the three plays specifically on lynching, this was the only one that met with the approval of all the FTP readers. ⟨. . .⟩ The clue to approval of *Sunday Morning* may be found in the reader's phrase "it is not offensive to either group." The persistent dilemma of which audience to address rears its head again, but sympathy for the characters seems to overcome the need to take sides and makes the play more acceptable. Subtextual statements on the hypocrisy of the Christian religion may also have touched sensitive chords in the readers' consciences. Nevertheless, the play was *not* given a production by The Federal Theatre Project.

Winona L. Fletcher, "From Genteel Poet to Revolutionary Playwright: Georgia Douglas Johnson," *Theatre Annual* 40 (1985): 52–53, 57–58

⊞ *Bibliography*

The Heart of a Woman and Other Poems. 1918.

Bronze: A Book of Verse. 1922.

Blue Blood. 1927.

Plumes. 1927.

An Autumn Love Cycle. 1928.

Share My World: A Book of Poems. 1962.

Claude McKay
1890–1948

CLAUDE MCKAY was born in Sunny Ville, Jamaica, on September 15, 1890. After being apprenticed to a wheelwright in Kingston, he emigrated to the U.S. in 1912 and studied agriculture at the Tuskegee Institute and at Kansas State University. He abandoned his studies in 1914 and moved to Harlem, where he became a leading radical poet. Before coming to America, McKay had published a collection of poetry entitled *Songs of Jamaica* (1912). While in Harlem he frequently wrote under the pseudonym Eli Edwards, a name derived from that of his wife, Eulalie Imelda Edwards. This marriage ended in 1914 after only six months; McKay's wife gave birth to a daughter whom he never saw.

"If We Must Die," perhaps McKay's best-known poem, was published in Max Eastman's magazine, the *Liberator*, in 1919. This stirring call to arms was written after the race riots that followed the end of World War I. McKay lived in London from 1919 to 1921; during this time he first read Karl Marx and worked for the Marxist periodical *Worker's Dreadnought*. In 1922—the year he published his celebrated poetry collection *Harlem Shadows*—he made a "magic pilgrimage" to the USSR, where he was warmly welcomed by the Communist leaders and addressed the Third Communist International. He wrote two works that were translated into Russian by P. Okhrimenko in 1923: *Sudom Lincha*, a collection of three stories, and the treatise *Negry v Amerike*. These works were translated into English by Robert Winter, the first (as *Trial by Lynching: Stories about Negro Life in America*) in 1977, the second (as *The Negroes in America*) in 1979. McKay's interest in Marxism seems to have been based on his perception of its calls for a return to agrarian values and for racial equality. However, McKay never joined the Communist party and by the 1930s he had completely renounced all association with communism.

From 1923 to 1934 McKay lived overseas, having left the United States as a result of his alienation from the black American intelligentsia and from the leaders of the Harlem Renaissance. In Paris he came to feel that racial barriers separated him from "the lost generation"; he subsequently moved to Marseilles and later to Morocco. In Marseilles he wrote his first two novels, *Home to Harlem* (1928) and *Banjo* (1929). On its publication, *Home to Harlem* became the most popular novel ever written by a black author. In 1932 McKay published a collection of short stories, *Gingertown*, followed by a third novel, *Banana Bottom* (1933).

Returning to the U.S. in 1934, McKay worked briefly as a laborer in a welfare camp. In 1937 he wrote *A Long Way from Home*, an account of his life since first coming to America. In 1944 he was baptized into the Roman Catholic church and wrote essays on Christian faith. He died in Chicago on May 22, 1948.

◈ *Critical Extracts*

JAMES WELDON JOHNSON McKay in 1911, when he was twenty, published a volume of verse, *Songs of Jamaica*. Most of the poems in this collection were written in the Jamaican dialect. It is important to note that these dialect poems of McKay are quite distinct in sentiment and treatment from the conventional Negro dialect poetry written by the poets in the United States; they are free from both the minstrel and plantation traditions, free from exaggerated sweetness and wholesomeness; they are veritable impressions of Negro life in Jamaica. Indeed, some of these dialect poems are decidedly militant in tone. It is, of course, clear to see that McKay had the advantage of not having to deal with stereotypes. He found his medium fresh and plastic. ⟨. . .⟩

McKay belongs to the post-war group and was its most powerful voice. He was preëminently the poet of the rebellion. More effectively than any other poet of that period he voiced the feelings and reactions the Negro in America was then experiencing. Incongruous as it seems, he chose as the form of these poems of protest, challenge, and defiance the English sonnet; and no poetry in American literature sounds a more portentous note than these sonnet-tragedies. Read "The Lynching" and note the final couplet:

> And little lads, lynchers that were to be,
> Danced around the dreadful thing in fiendish glee.

The terrifying summer of 1919, when race riots occurred in quick succes-
sion in a dozen cities in different sections of the country, brought from him
the most widely known of these sonnets, a cry of defiant desperation,
beginning with the lines:

> If we must die—let it not be like hogs
> Hunted and penned in an inglorious spot,

and closing with:

> Like men we'll face the murderous, cowardly pack,
> Pressed to the wall, dying, but fighting back!

This is masculine poetry, strong and direct, the sort of poetry that stirs
the pulse, that quickens to action. Reading McKay's poetry of protest and
rebellion, it is difficult to imagine him dreaming of his native Jamaica and
singing as he does in "Flame Heart" or creating poetic beauty in the absolute
as he does in "The Harlem Dancer," "Spring in New Hampshire," and many
another of his poems. Of the major Negro poets he, above all, is the poet
of passion. That passion found in his poems of rebellion, transmuted, is felt
in his love lyrics.

James Weldon Johnson, *The Book of American Negro Poetry* (New York: Harcourt,
Brace & World, 1922), pp. 165–67

WALTER F. WHITE   With the publication of *Harlem Shadows* by
Claude McKay we are introduced to the work of a man who shows very
genuine poetical promise. His work proves him to be a craftsman with
keen perception of emotions, a lover of the colorful and dramatic, strongly
sensuous yet never sensual, and an adept in the handling of his phrases to
give the subtle variations of thought he seeks. He has mastered the forms
of the lyric and the sonnet—in fact, there is in this volume perhaps too
much sameness of form. Yet one can have no quarrel with a man who works
in that medium in which he is most at home, and I do not quarrel with
Mr. McKay for sticking to these modes of expression.

I wish that I had the ability to convey the sheer delight which this book
of verse gives me. Keenly sensitive to color and beauty and tragedy and
mirth, he does, as Max Eastman says in his introduction, cause us to "find
our literature vividly enriched by a voice from this most alien race among

us." Mr. McKay is most compelling when he voices his protest against the wrongs inflicted on his people, yet in his love lyrics there is a beauty and a charm that reveal the true poetic gift.

Walter F. White, "Negro Poets," *Nation*, 7 June 1922, pp. 694–95

WALLACE THURMAN   McKay's first volume was published while he was still in Jamaica, a compilation of folk verse done in the native dialect. The Institute of Arts and Sciences of Jamaica gave him a medal in recognition of this first book. It is in many ways remarkable, and in it the poet gives us a more substantial portrait and delves deeper into the soul of the Jamaican than Dunbar was ever able to in the soul of the southern Negro in America.

McKay's latter poetry is often marred by bombast. He is such an intense person that one can often hear the furnace-like fire within him roaring in his poems. He seems to have more emotional depth and spiritual fire than any of his forerunners or contemporaries. It might be added that he also seems to have considerably more mental depth too. His love poems are not as musical or as haunting as Mr. Cullen's, but neither are they as stereotyped. His sonnet to a Harlem dancer may not be as deft or as free from sentiment as "Midnight Man" by Langston Hughes, but it is far more mature and moving. All of which leads us to say that a study of Claude McKay's and of the better Negro poetry convinces us that he, more than the rest, has really had something to say. It is his tragedy that his message was too alive and too big for the form he chose. His poems could never shape the flames from the fire that blazed within him. But he is the only Negro poet who ever wrote revolutionary or protest poetry.

Wallace Thurman, "Negro Poets and their Poetry," *Bookman* (New York): 67, No. 5 (July 1928): 559

CLAUDE McKAY   A negro writer feeling the urge to write faithfully about the people he knows from real experience and impartial observation is caught in a dilemma (unless he possesses a very strong sense of esthetic values) between the opinion of this group and his own artistic consciousness. I have read pages upon pages of denunciation of young Negro poets and story-tellers who were trying to grasp and render the significance of the background, the fundamental rhythm of Aframerican life. But not a line of critical encouragement for the artistic exploitation of the homely things— of Maudy's wash tub, Aunt Jemima's white folks, Miss Ann's old clothes for work-and-wages, George's Yessah-boss, dining car and Pullman services, barber and shoe shine shop, chittling and corn-pone joints—all the lowly things that go to the formation of the Aframerican soil in which the best, the most pretentious of Aframerican society still has its roots.

My own experience has been amazing. Before I published *Home to Harlem* I was known to the Negro public as the writer of the hortatory poem "If We Must Die." This poem was written during the time of the Chicago race riots. I was then a train waiter in the service of the Pennsylvania Railroad. Our dining car was running between New York, Philadelphia and Pittsburgh, Harrisburg and Washington and I remember we waiters and cooks carried revolvers in secret and always kept together going from our quarters to the railroad yards, as a precaution against sudden attack.

The poem was an outgrowth of the intense emotional experience I was living through (no doubt with thousands of other Negroes) in those days. It appeared in the radical magazine the *Liberator*, and was widely reprinted in the Negro press. Later it was included in my book of poetry *Harlem Shadows*. At the time I was writing a great deal of lyric poetry and none of my colleagues on the *Liberator* considered me a propaganda poet who could reel off revolutionary poetry like an automatic machine cutting fixed patterns. If we were a rebel group because we had faith that human life might be richer, by the same token we believed in the highest standards of creative work.

"If We Must Die" immediately won popularity among Aframericans, but the tone of the Negro critics was apologetic. To them a poem that voiced the deep-rooted instinct of self-preservation seemed merely a daring piece of impertinence. The dean of Negro critics ⟨William Stanley Braithwaite⟩ denounced me as a "violent and angry propagandist, using his natural poetic gifts to clothe arrogant and defiant thoughts." A young disciple characterized me as "rebellious and vituperative."

Thus it seems that respectable Negro opinion and criticism are not ready for artistic or other iconoclasm in Negroes. Between them they would emasculate the colored literary aspirant. Because Aframerican group life is possible only on a neutral and negative level our critics are apparently under the delusion that an Aframerican literature and art may be created out of evasion and insincerity.

Claude McKay, "A Negro Writer to His Critics" (1932), *The Passion of Claude McKay: Selected Poetry and Prose 1912–1948*, ed. Wayne F. Cooper (New York: Schocken Books, 1973), pp. 133–34

J. SAUNDERS REDDING   It was Mr. McKay's third volume of poetry, *Harlem Shadows*, that attracted his darker audience most. In this volume he gives voice to the violence and bitter hatred that marked the interracial strife of the period just after the war. The proud defiance and independence that were the very heart of the new Negro movement is nowhere so strikingly expressed in poetry as in "To the White Friends" and in "If We Must Die" ⟨. . .⟩

Despite the awakening of a new artistic consciousness, however, there was at first much confusion in the new Negro movement in literature. The great tide of feeling which found release was not directed through one channel. While Claude McKay spat out his proud impatience, a few were indulging in slapstick, trying in song and story (and with the aid of certain popular white writers) to restore the older tradition to a state of health, and other writers were groping with curious shyness through the teeming byways of racial thought and feeling, searching for an alchemy, a universal solvent for transmuting the passions of the day into something sweeter than bitterness, more pure than hate. They were for the most part older writers who had an hereditary confidence in the essential goodness of man, in the theory of American democracy, and in the Victorian notion that

> God's in his heaven;
> All's right with the world.

They were of the comfortable middle classes, the bourgeois, school teachers, the wives of pork-fattened politicians and ministers, the sons of headwaiters and porters, spiritually far removed from the sources of new race thought. McKay, Toomer, Hughes, and the numerous lesser ones who came later were vagabonds, as free in the sun and dust of Georgia, in the steerage of tramp steamers, in the brothels of Lenox Avenue and the crowded ports of the Orient as in the living rooms of Strivers Row. These were the reservoirs through which pumped the race's hate power, love power, lust power, laugh power. The others, the conservatives, were tubs without depth, within whose narrow limits no storm could be raised.

> J. Saunders Redding, *To Make a Poet Black* (Chapel Hill: University of North Carolina Press, 1939), pp. 102–3

ROBERT A. SMITH   One must admit that the author's most power-ful dudgeon lay in this protest poetry. Whether he wrote an epigram, a sonnet, or a longer poem, his thought is sustained. He expressed the deepest resentment, but even when doing so his feelings were lucid. He did not stumble as he attempted to express himself. This dynamic force within his poetry caused him to be constantly read and re-read by his admirers and critics. They realized that here was a man of deepest emotions, as well as one who was a skilled craftsman.

In the sonnet, McKay had found a verse form peculiarly adaptable to his taste and ability. His talent was diversified, but this form with its rise and fall seemed quite the thing for the thought which he wished to convey to his readers. Sonnets that bear out this idea are "America," "If We Must Die," and "The Lynching." "America" does not show McKay's bitterness. It gives advice to Negro Americans to face squarely the tests and the challenges that come to them as a persecuted minority. "If We Must Die" reflects the author's acrimony toward the lynchers of Negroes. Written during the epidemic of race riots which swept the country in 1919, its theme is: "fight back; do not take a beating lying down".

Other poems which in content are racial protest are: "In Bondage," "Outcast," "The White City," and the "Barrier." The rebellious philosophy in McKay may be traced back through his turbulent youth, and his affiliation with radical organizations and people.

Occasionally, however, one sees another side of McKay. When he puts down his rancor, his lyricism is entirely clear. He paints pictures that are beautiful; especially is this true when he describes scenes of his native islands. One sees in the poet a sort of nostalgia for home, for relatives, and for the scenes of childhood days, long past. It is in this idyllic mood that McKay appears in an entirely different light. Possibly one of the best poems of this sort is "Flame-Heart." It contains beautiful lines of description such as "The poinsettia's red, blood red in warm December," and "Sweet with the golden threads of the rose apple." "To One Coming North" and "The Tropics in

New York" are in the same vein. Although not concerned with the West Indies, they do picture scenes of nature and peacefulness. Their mood is one of quietness also. Others in this group show McKay's range and facility. There is sheer delight in reading them, and the collection would be richer with more of the same tone. ⟨. . .⟩

McKay took upon himself a tremendous task when he chose to be the leading spokesman of an oppressed race. The question always arises as to whether a poet loses any or all of his effectiveness when he takes upon his shoulders the problem of fighting. Does one's lyrical ability become clouded by his propaganda or bombast? is another question. This, it seems, may or may not be true. In the case of McKay, what he has had to say, for the most part has been important. Literary history is full of humanitarians who attacked conditions that were unsavory. Some were successful in their attacks; others were not. Although he was frequently concerned with the race problem, his style is basically lucid. One feels disinclined to believe that the medium which he chose was too small, or too large for his message. He has been heard.

> Robert A. Smith, "Claude McKay: An Essay in Criticism," *Phylon* 9, No. 3 (September 1948): 272–73

ARTHUR D. DRAYTON   Outside Jamaican and Negro literary circles in the United States, the late Jamaican poet, Claude McKay, is known best and often only for his race-conscious verse, sometimes only by his much-quoted sonnet which Sir Winston Churchill helped to popularize during World War II. For many people, in the same way that 'The Negro Speaks of Rivers' is Langston Hughes, so this particular sonnet is McKay.

> If we must die, let it not be like hogs
> Hunted and penned in an inglorious spot,
> While round us bark the mad and hungry dogs,
> Making their mock at our accursed lot.
> If we must die, O let us nobly die,
> So that our precious blood may not be shed
> In vain; then even the monsters we defy
> Shall be constrained to honor us though dead!
> O kinsmen! we must meet the common foe!
> Though far outnumbered let us show us brave,
> And for their thousand blows deal one deathblow!

What though before us lies the open grave?
Like men we'll face the murderous, cowardly pack,
Pressed to the wall, dying, but fighting back!

G. R. Coulthard has described his protest verse as 'bitter and violent', and has observed that 'his best poems are characterised by a racial hatred, or even a challenge, of the most violent kind'. Bitter and violent; a challenge: yes. But the charge of racial hatred is difficult to support; and unless we are to argue a complete change in McKay between this later protest verse and his earlier dialect poems, it is a strange assertion. For, quite apart from the evidence of the protest verse itself, it assumes a new dimension if one is familiar with McKay's two publications of dialect poems before he left Jamaica to take up residence in the United States.

But it is not surprising that McKay should have won recognition through his verse written around the theme of Negro suffering in the States. For this has the virility one might expect of a Caribbean poet shocked by what he discovers in America. Coming from quite a different kind of experience of Negro degradation in Jamaica, McKay was fired by what he saw in the States and helped to give to American Negro poetry a distinctly different voice.

⟨. . .⟩ McKay's early years in America coincided with crucial years for the Negro cause, and the virility of his verse was in keeping with the prevailing atmosphere. But, looked at closely, this virility reveals itself as based on something more than mere bitterness; it includes and depends on a certain resilience—perhaps stubborn humanity would be better—on the part of the poet. And this in turn is to be traced to McKay's capacity to react to Negro suffering, not just as a Negro, but as a human being; to react to human suffering as such. For there is a certain danger which is inherent in the Negro situation, one which can lead to great human tragedy, and has no doubt done so times without number in individual cases. It is that the Negro, because of the injustices which he has suffered and continues to suffer, reacts quite rightly as a Negro to the degradation of the Negro; but he is called upon to react in this way so continually, and at times so violently, that he is in danger of losing his capacity to react to suffering in a way which rises above this and includes it, to react simply and primarily as a human being. White bigotry has become so insistent that it is difficult to ask this of the Negro, and he is left in danger of not being touched by human suffering outside the Negro context, or outside a situation which closely resembles his own. And yet, if he is not to abdicate his humanity, he must retain his capacity for this larger and more basic reaction, since to be without it has frightful implications for his emotional growth and his stature as a human being.

For the poet, especially one handling 'racial' material, to lack it would be anathema. If he does not have it, he may as well go off and write about daffodils and lakes. But if by identifying himself with his own community or race he can proceed to that greater and more meaningful identification based on his humanity, he is qualified to handle 'racial' material. McKay always had this qualification, and it imparted to his verse a certain universal significance. Thus the sonnet 'If We Must Die' was written after and relates to the Washington race riot of 1919. Sir Winston Churchill, however, could use it to whip up defiant courage during World War II because it is essentially a cry of defiance from the human heart in the face of a threat to man's dignity and civilisation, a threat which was and is true of Nazism and the hatred of the Negro alike.

Arthur D. Drayton, "McKay's Human Pity: A Note on His Poetry," *Black Orpheus* No. 17 (June 1965): 39–40

DAVID LITTLEJOHN   Claude McKay, as a poet, is most kindly served by reading a few of his strongest poems, or even selected lines. The more thoroughly one studies his work, the more disagreeably McKay is revealed as the small-souled declamatory propagandist we meet in his novels. The best poems from his angry series of race-war sonnets ("Baptism," "If We Must Die," "Outcast," "Like a Strong Tree," "The White House") convey a bitter, masculine, very personal strength, a kind of enlightened crimson rant: the man who loves to hate, and has objects worth hating.

There is nothing new or experimental about his efforts. At its best (or at the reader's most tolerant) his work seems to have a kind of harsh, proud seventeenth-century vigor, like Milton's sonnet "On the Late Massacre in Piedmont" ("Avenge, O Lord, thy slaughtered saints"). From another point of view, though, the diction may be seen as a kind of archaic British bluster ("O let us nobly die," "Kinsmen," "bend the knee," "clime," "making their mock at our accursed lot"); the best-known of his poems was once quoted by Churchill.

His strength *is* in his anger, in the fury of his rhythms and images and diction; his weakness lies in his smallmindedness and poetic inability. He writes in chunky, aggressively iambic, end-stopped pentameters, deep-chested rhetorical lines of accusation and defiance, full of mouth-filling vowels and chopped consonants. He will make a dozen bad mistakes per sonnet, and dip to all forms of archaism and syntactic ineptitude to crash his way out of a poem ("From dulcet thoughts of you my guts are twisted"). Looked at too closely, the ideas behind his angry rhetoric often show as incoherent black-racist propaganda. He is not a pleasant sort.

> David Littlejohn, *Black on White: A Critical Survey of Writing by American Negroes* (New York: Grossman Publishers, 1966), pp. 56–57

ADDISON GAYLE, JR.   The theme of "The Outcast" is the disharmony between body and spirit occasioned by the imprisonment of the body and the culture plunder of the spirit. Slavery, in imprisoning the body, forced the spirit to dwell in a house of bondage where words were felt but never heard; and jungle songs which might have been sung were too soon forgotten in the face of cultural genocide. Thus, a silence was imposed upon the spirit, old cultural artifacts were destroyed, cultural ties were ripped asunder and truth and creativity distorted and stifled.

McKay foresees our continuing dilemma: Nothing is changed, because the form of slavery has undergone alteration during the twentieth century. The chains have been replaced by segregationist rules and laws, and cultural disintegration is almost complete. A view of the world which depicts Western Civilization—its institutions and culture—as the *sine qua non* of human achievement has become part of the mental equipage of each Black spirit. In the house of bondage where the Black body lies prostrate, the eternal note still sounds: whiteness is divine, Blackness is evil.

This was not purely an American phenomenon. Africans too learned to devaluate themselves, to wage war on one another as a result of European value judgments. In America, a subconscious wish to be white precipitated internecine warfare between Black men of different skin color, between educated and uneducated Blacks, between poor and not so poor Blacks. By the middle of the twentieth century, Blacks the world over were singing the universal song: Thou shalt have no god or culture other than that vouchsafed by the Western world.

Against this cultural arrogance, the African poets of Negritude leveled their artistic guns. Their objective was to reverse the trend among Africans of accepting what McKay called "alien gods." The people had to undergo a de-brainwashing; they had to recreate the symbols and myths of the past, and in so doing, arrive once again at a level of self-comprehension. It is, in this regard, no surprise that the Negritude poets borrowed extensively from their counterparts of the Harlem Renaissance, who were waging their own battle against the symbols and images imposed upon their people.

"The Outcast" may be seen, therefore, as a theoretical link between the poets of Negritude and the poets of the Harlem Renaissance, even if it foreshadows the poets of Cultural Nationalism. At the core of each movement is the desire of Black men to express "their dark-skinned selves," unimpeded by the cultural dictates of the white Western world. These poets are one with McKay in the assertion that ". . . the great western world holds me in fee, / And I may never hope for full release / While to its alien gods I bend my knee." And across the boundaries of time and geography, they cry out with the same intense dedication and desperation: "For I was born, far from my native clime / Under the white man's menace, out of time."

Returning, then, with McKay to other times, when Western images and symbols were not so well solidified in the Black psyche, when Black men did not believe that their manifest destiny was to be changed into white men, when a people—from the jungles of Timbuctu to the streets of Harlem—was conscious of their beauty and self worth—returning to such times, Black poets have sought to make their impact throughout the world. The function of such poetry is, beyond a doubt, revolutionary, and it is in this sense that *Harlem Shadows* is a revolutionary document and Claude McKay is a revolutionary poet. He is the militant poet, the angry poet, the poet who calls for revolutionary action.

Addison Gayle, Jr., *Claude McKay: The Black Poet at War* (Detroit: Broadside Press, 1972), pp. 37–39

JAMES R. GILES   For a final evaluation of Claude McKay the poet, it is useful to turn to Melvin B. Tolson's review of *Selected Poems* (in *Poetry*, February 1954). To Tolson, the "logic of facts" separated McKay and other Harlem Renaissance poets from "the New Poetry and Criticism" of the 1920s. The work of Jean Toomer seems to bring this generalization into question; and, to the degree that "the New Poetry and Criticism" simply implied innovation and rejection of restrictive and traditional poetic form and language, so would that of Langston Hughes. But Tolson is correct about Claude McKay, for his poetry does seem to have come from a different world than the work of Pound, Cummings, and Stevens—and, in fact, it did. By the "logic of facts," one assumes that Tolson is referring to McKay's special burdens of protest against white oppression, to the virtual absence of Afro-American poetic tradition, and to McKay's lifelong allegiance to British literary traditions of the nineteenth century. McKay had to be concerned with expressing a black anger against injustice and with creating something to replace the dialect verse of Paul Dunbar. Radical innovation in form was not, then, one of McKay's concerns; in fact, he was suspicious of it. As mentioned, one often wishes that it had been different and that McKay could have seen a correlation between technical innovation in poetry and blackness. But the facts are, as Tolson says, that ". . . McKay's radicalism was in content—not in form." Still, the "content" of McKay's specifically black poetry was instrumental in shattering "the mould of the Dialect School and the Booker T. Washington compromise."

Though Tolson never directly says so, one assumes Tolson is implying that McKay's kind of "radicalism" made it easier for the later Afro-American poets who were concerned with the "New Poetry"—and because Tolson himself is a prime example of the post-Renaissance innovators, his review of Selected Poems is a significant tribute to the writer of "If We Must Die." The McKay heritage to black poetry is then doubly meaningful: his rebellion against the plantation school resulted in a liberation whose dimensions he did not foresee. In the 1940s, Tolson's artistic world was not so alien from that of Pound and Cummings; and Ishmael Reed completes, of course, the movement into experimentation. What McKay undoubtedly did hope for, if not foresee, was the angry black poetry of Baraka and Lee; and his contribution to that school is clear.

Apart from McKay's overtly black poetic contribution, there is more: some interesting proletarian verse, expressions of spiritual anguish, and some fine metaphysical love poetry, for example. The best of the poems in "Amoroso" have never been sufficiently appreciated. Finally, in "St. Isaac's Church, Petrograd," McKay developed an intriguing concept of the relationship between art, religion, and human suffering; and the several dimensions of his personality and interests had positive aesthetic results.

In his novels, he was able to be revolutionary in both form and content. When he wrote Banana Bottom, he reached the peak of his literary promise. For that reason, the three novels are ultimately more rewarding than the poetry. Nonetheless, *Selected Poems* is both a landmark of Afro-American writing and evidence of an ability to handle with success diverse themes and subject matter. *Harlem Shadows* was the book which firmly established McKay as a Harlem Renaissance figure. Unlike *Home to Harlem*, it pleased virtually everyone in the Renaissance establishment. Obviously, for several key people, an unrealistically limited perception of Claude McKay resulted from it. Partly because of that misconception, the book gave its author a position of influence in the Negro literary movement of the 1920s which he might well not otherwise have held.

James R. Giles, *Claude McKay* (Boston: Twayne, 1976), pp. 67–68

WAYNE F. COOPER   Despite his genuine achievements in *Songs of Jamaica* and *Constab Ballads*, these volumes too often betrayed McKay's literary inexperience, emotional confusion, and intellectual immaturity. In "Bennie's Departure," a long description of his affection for and emotional dependence on a fellow recruit in the early days of their enlistment—a description, not incidentally, that bordered upon a passionate declaration of homosexual love—McKay observed that Bennie "was always quick and steady, / Not of wav'rin' min' like me." McKay's "wav'rin' min' " can in part be attributed to his youthful inexperience and in part to the deep-seated psychological insecurity with which he viewed his future. But his uncertainty was made even more acute by his ambivalent suspension at this stage of his life between the peasant culture and the literate colonial society. All these factors contributed to the stylistic problems and contradictory emotional and intellectual stances in his dialect poetry.

Despite his emotional loyalty to the Jamaican peasantry, his commitment to the dialect was not total because he could not adequately express through his dialect persona all those aspects of his own intellectual and literary experiences that he had assimilated as an educated colonial. His education claimed a part of his being as surely as did his peasant heritage and could not be denied expression, as its awkward manifestation in the dialect attested. Although tied emotionally and racially to the uneducated peasantry, he no longer fully shared their necessarily restricted world view. On the other hand, while sharing the literate consciousness of the race from whom he had acquired his education, he could not identify with it at the deepest levels of his emotions.

Given this dual estrangement, the wonder is not that so much of McKay's dialect poetry was bad but that he achieved in it as much as he did. In his later poetry and novels, he would handle the problems of alienation and identity with greater self-consciousness and with more sophistication.

Wayne F. Cooper, *Claude McKay: Rebel Sojourner in the Harlem Renaissance* (Baton Rouge: Louisiana State University Press, 1987), pp. 46–47

P. S. CHAUHAN   Linguistically, his work bears the mark all too common to the writing done in colonies. It is pulled by two gravitational forces: the one of his native tongue, the other of the language of the colonizer. In his first book of poems published in the United States, *Harlem Shadows* (1922), McKay confesses to the linguistic tension that had been part of his upbringing. "The speech of my childhood and early youth," he writes, "was the Jamaica dialect ... which still preserves a few words of African origin, and which is more difficult of understanding than the American Negro dialect. But the language we wrote and read in school was England's English." The dual versions of the language, like those of the island culture, internalized during the period of his cognitive development, haunt McKay's work to the very end and affect its tone and texture in various ways.

His earliest poems, *Songs of Jamaica* (1912), were proclaimed to be dialect poetry, which, in the main, they were. In the poetic pieces there is, however, something besides dialect at work, as is seen, for example, in his poem "Whe' Fe Do?" Note the fifth stanza of the poem:

> We've go to wuk wid might an' main,
> To us we ha' an' use we brain,
> To toil an' worry, 'cheme and 'train
> Fe t'ings that bring more loss dan gain;
> To stan' de sun an' bear de rain,
> An' suck we bellyful o'pain
> Widouten cry nor yet complain—
> For dat caan' [won't] do.

It is significant that if there is a vernacular grammar at work in the line "widouten cry nor yet complain," there is a literary and a balanced line as well ("to toil and worry, scheme and train"), a line, by the way, with a caesura, too. A purely native expression, "to suck a bellyful of pain," is similarly relieved by a perfectly English phrase, "to work with might and main."

The split between the two versions of English goes deeper, however, than it may appear at first. The fourth line has, for example, a perfectly good English "that," but the eighth line reverts to the dialectical "dat." And there is another word, too, which in its journey through the stanza undergoes a similar transformation between the fourth and eighth lines. Whereas the fourth begins with "Fe," the eighth opens with the normal "For." Lexical loyalties of the poet, the stanza bears out, are about evenly divided between the native dialect and the metropolitan English. Even as he seeks to embody the experience of a farm laborer, McKay gets enticed by the idiom of the Master, by the privileged language of the dominant group, betraying the inroads of the colonizer's influence.

> P. S. Chauhan, "Rereading Claude McKay," *CLA Journal* 34, No. 1 (September 1990): 72–73

MICHEL FABRE   Of all the Afro-American writers who resided in France between the two world wars, Claude McKay remained there the longest and mixed most with all sorts of people—black and white, American and French, European and African—in both Paris and the provinces. He also derived inspiration from his French experience, not only in *Banjo*, in which Marseilles plays more than a background role, but in a number of essays analyzing the complex class and race relations in Western Europe. If Countee Cullen and Langston Hughes also went beyond the tourist stage when they lived in Paris, because of his deeper political awareness McKay proved to be more discriminating than Cullen in his likes and dislikes, less superficial than Hughes in rendering French ways of life and the Paris atmosphere, and more sophisticated than either in his views about the colonial situation and the black diaspora. ⟨. . .⟩

When he first set foot in France, McKay was well aware of its politics and its role in colonizing Africa. As early as 1920 he had written the editors of the London *Daily World* to protest the bourgeois press coverage of the use of black occupation troops by the French in the Rhineland: the "black threat" had been made into a question of potential miscegenation. But, McKay thought, defending the morality of the Negro race mattered less than understanding that, by helping French capitalism to hold Germany

down, the black troops were supporting France's dominion in Africa. He
was also quick to denounce French racism. He was convinced that, in spite
of appearances, Senegalese Blaise Diagne had undermined W. E. B. Du
Bois's efforts at the 1919 Pan-African Conference in Paris: hadn't Diagne
declared that French blacks should consider themselves Frenchmen, not
colored internationalists, for "the position of Negro citizens in France [was]
truly worthy of envy"? Yet even such an active supporter of assimilation as
Diagne, McKay noted, had been forced to concede that French whites
denied the black man even mere physical equality: the victory of Senegalese
boxer Battling Siki over native Frenchman Georges Charpentier for the
world championship had created no less a scandal than that of Jack Johnson
over Australian Tommy Burns. Even before seeing France, McKay could
thus provide a sophisticated analysis of race prejudice there and of the pro-
French attitude of the gullible Afro-American intelligentsia:

> The good treatment of individuals by those whom they meet in
> France is valued so highly by Negroes that they are beginning to
> forget about the exploitation of Africans by the French. . . . Thus
> the sympathy of the Negro intelligentsia is completely on the side
> of France. It is well-informed about the barbarous acts of the
> Belgians in the Congo but it knows nothing at all about the
> barbarous acts of the French in Senegal, about the organized
> robbery of native workers, about the forced enlistment of recruits,
> about the fact that the population is reduced to extreme poverty
> and hunger, or about the total annihilation of tribes. It is possible
> that the Negro intelligentsia does not want to know about all
> this, inasmuch as it can loosely generalize about the differences in
> the treatment of Negroes in bourgeois France and in plutocratic
> America. René Maran wrote a novel which, by the way, is an
> indignant denunciation of the activities of the French government
> in Africa; but the author, in spite of this, received the Goncourt
> prize and indisputably became a desired member of writers' and
> artists' circles in France. Dr. Du Bois writes a surprisingly moving
> work, *The Souls of Black Folk,* written in splendid English;
> nevertheless, he remains up to the present an outcast in
> American society.

This set the tone for McKay's lasting attitude concerning the myth of
French liberalism: although he enjoyed genuine friendships with a number
of individual French people, he always refused to exonerate French institu-
tions and culture from responsibility for their colonial oppression.
Michel Fabre, *From Harlem to Paris: Black American Writers in France 1840–1980*
(Urbana: University of Illinois Press, 1991), pp. 92–94

TYRONE TILLERY   The black community's embrace of "If We Must Die" as its own is wholly understandable. America's entry into World War I had summoned black Americans to a supreme challenge: to "close ranks" with white Americans to save the world for democracy, while temporarily putting aside their own historic grievances. How could America launch a crusade to destroy tyranny and spread democracy throughout the world without providing justice for the black millions in America during the postwar period? But before the war had even ended, in East St. Louis, Houston, and countless other places, the black hope of full citizenship was dashed to bits. W. E. B. Du Bois, whose *Crisis* editorial "Close Ranks" had been most responsible for rallying the African-American community to the national cause, now on May 7, 1919, urged blacks "to fight a sterner, longer, more unbending battle against the forces of hell in our own land." But even the *Crisis* editor's exhortatory words,

> We return
> We return from fighting.
> We return fighting

could not express the emotions African Americans felt: anger, disillusionment, protest, and challenge. McKay's sonnet, though seemingly an incongruous medium for pouring out cynicism and bitterness, was not compromised as Du Bois had been in his "Returning Soldiers." Moreover, Max Eastman may have been correct in his critical estimation that McKay was a great lyric genius of his race. In "If We Must Die" that genius satisfied what sociologist Horace Cayton has described as "a deep hunger in the hearts of more than a million American Negroes," in the postwar period. The poem was reprinted in black magazines and newspapers and established McKay as "a poet of his people." It was committed to memory; recited at school exercises and public meetings; and discussed at private gatherings. Its impact as a harbinger and symbol of a transition in black letters continued to affect black writers even a generation after it first appeared. Writer M. Carl Holman remembers that during his high school years he yearned to write a poem as defiantly bitter as McKay's "If We Must Die."

Cedric Dover, McKay's close friend, struck a note of profound truth when he remarked, "Ironies are the ways of history." While McKay appreciated the honor bestowed upon him by the black community, he was nonetheless uncomfortable at being cast in the role of a race poet representing the African American. As he put it, "And for it ["If We Must Die"] the Negro people unanimously hailed me as a poet. Indeed, that one grand outburst is their sole standard of my poetry." Such praise, he feared, bordered on racial patronage and not on appreciation of his ability as a poet and intellectual. What he desired most in 1919 was to be the "individual soul" who sought what was noblest and best in the life of the individual. He put his faith in the maxim "each soul must save itself," which had expressed his approach to life and literature since his boyhood days in Jamaica.

Tyrone Tillery, *Claude McKay: A Black Poet's Struggle for Identity* (Amherst: University of Massachusetts Press, 1992), pp. 36–37

❖ *Bibliography*

Songs of Jamaica. 1912.

Constab Ballads. 1912.

Spring in New Hampshire and Other Poems. 1920.

Harlem Shadows. 1922.

Sudom Lincha. Tr. P. Okhrimenko. 1923.

Negry v Amerike. Tr. P. Okhrimenko. 1923.

Home to Harlem. 1928.

Banjo: A Story without a Plot. 1929.

Gingertown. 1932.

Banana Bottom. 1933.

A Long Way from Home. 1937.

Harlem: Negro Metropolis. 1940.

Selected Poems. 1953.

The Dialect Poetry. 1972.

The Passion of Claude McKay: Selected Prose and Poetry 1912–1948. Ed. Wayne F. Cooper. 1973.

My Green Hills of Jamaica and Five Jamaican Short Stories. 1979.

Jean Toomer
1894–1967

JEAN TOOMER was born Nathan Pinchback Toomer in Washington, D.C., on December 26, 1894, the son of Nathan and Nina Pinchback Toomer. At his grandfather's insistence he was called Eugene Toomer, and later he adopted the first name Jean because he thought it had a more literary connotation. Nathan Toomer abandoned the family soon after Jean was born, and Nina Toomer, after living with her parents for some years, moved in 1906 to New Rochelle, New York, where she lived with her white husband. She died in 1909, and Jean returned to Washington to live with his grandparents. At this time his grandfather, P. B. S. Pinchback, informed Toomer—who looked white and believed himself to be white—that he was of racially mixed ancestry.

Toomer attended several universities between 1914 and 1919, including the University of Wisconsin and the City College of New York, but finally abandoned academic life to pursue literature, writing poetry and fiction for such magazines as the *Little Review*, *Secession*, and *Broom*. Toomer disliked the use of race labels, insisting he was neither white nor black but "simply an American." He held the belief that race was not a fundamental constituent in one's self-definition, and was accordingly criticized for the lack of a black focus in his later works.

Toomer is best remembered for his first book, *Cane* (1923), a miscellany of stories, verse, and a drama concerned with the lives of black Americans in the United States. Much of the source material for this work was derived from a trip to Georgia he took in the fall of 1921. *Cane* is now regarded as one of the most remarkable novels of its time because of its prose-poetic language, its amalgamation of literary genres, and its rich evocation of the lives of both northern and southern black Americans.

Toomer's other works are the plays *Balo*, *Natalie Mann*, and *The Sacred Factory*; the novella "York Beach" (1929); *Essentials* (1931), a collection of aphorisms; the 800-line poem "The Blue Meridian" (1936), a radical expansion of an earlier poem entitled "The First American"; and other stories, essays, and poems. Many of these works, as well as a selection from his autobiographical writings, have been gathered in *The Wayward and the Seeking: A Collection of Writings by Jean Toomer* (1980), edited by Darwin Turner. Several novels, plays, and stories remain unpublished.

In the mid-1920s Toomer became interested in the work of the mystic Georges Ivanovitch Gurdjieff. Gurdjieff's philosophy stressed the union of physical, mental, and psychological functions to achieve inner harmony, and Toomer taught the Gurdjieff method between 1925 and 1933. In 1931 he resided in a communal arrangement with eight unmarried male and female friends in Portage, Wisconsin; later he married one of the participants, Margery Latimer, who died while giving birth to their only child. Alternative spiritual disciplines obsessed Toomer, who devoted himself successively to Quakerism and to L. Ron Hubbard's Scientology. It is frequently asserted that Toomer's devotion to Gurdjieff, Scientology, and other pseudoscientific religions ruined him as a writer, as it made his later work dogmatic and excessively didactic.

In 1934 Toomer married again, this time to Marjorie Content, whose father gave the couple a farm in Bucks County, Pennsylvania. Aside from a trip to India in 1939, Toomer lived in seclusion on the farm, writing little and suffering increasing health problems. He died on March 30, 1967.

▣ Critical Extracts

WALDO FRANK   Reading his book ⟨*Cane*⟩, I had the vision of a land, heretofore sunk in the mists of muteness, suddenly rising up into the eminence of song. Innumerable books have been written about the South; some good books have been written about the South. This book *is* the South. I do not mean that *Cane* covers the South or is the South's full voice. Merely this: a poet has arisen among our American youth who has known how to turn the essences and materials of his Southland into the essences and materials of literature. A poet has arisen in that land who writes, not as a Southerner, not as a rebel against Southerners, not as a Negro, not as apologist or priest or critic: who writes as a *poet*. The fashioning of beauty is ever foremost in his inspiration: not forcedly but simply, and because these ultimate aspects of his world are to him more real than all its specific problems. He has made songs and lovely stories of his land . . . not of its yesterday, but of its immediate life. And that has been enough. ⟨. . .⟩

How typical is *Cane* of the South's still virgin soil and of its pressing seeds! and the book's chaos of verse, tale, drama, its rhythmic rolling shift from lyricism to narrative, from mystery to intimate pathos! But read the book through and you will see a complex and significant form take substance from its chaos. Part One is the primitive and evanescent black world of Georgia. Part Two is the threshing and suffering brown world of Washington, lifted by opportunity and contact into the anguish of self-conscious struggle. Part Three is Georgia again . . . the invasion into this black womb of the ferment seed: the neurotic, educated, spiritually stirring Negro. As a broad form this is superb, and the very looseness and unexpected waves of the book's parts make *Cane* still more *South*, still more of an esthetic equivalent of the land.

     Waldo Frank, "Foreword [to the 1923 edition of *Cane*]," *Cane* by Jean Toomer(New
     York: W. W. Norton, 1988), pp. 138–40

GORHAM B. MUNSON   There can be no question of Jean Toomer's skill as a literary craftsman. A writer who can combine vowels and liquids to form a cadence like "she was as innocently lovely as a November cotton flower" has a subtle command of word-music. And a writer who can break the boundaries of the sentences, interrupt the placement of a fact with a lyrical cry, and yet hold both his fact and his exclamation to a single welded meaning as in the expression: "A single room held down to earth . . . O fly away to Jesus . . . by a leaning chimney . . .", is assuredly at home in the language and therefore is assuredly free to experiment and invent. Toomer has found his own speech, now swift and clipped for violent narrative action, now languorous and dragging for specific characterizing purposes, and now lean and sinuous for the exposition of ideas, but always cadenced to accord with an unusually sensitive ear.

It is interesting to know that Toomer, before he began to write, thought of becoming a composer. One might have guessed it from the fact that the early sketches in *Cane* (1923) depend fully as much upon a musical unity as upon a literary unity. "Karintha," for example, opens with a song, presents a theme, breaks into song, develops the theme, sings again, drops back into prose, and dies away in a song. But in it certain narrative functions—one might mention that lying back of the bald statement, "This interest of the male, who wishes to ripen a growing thing too soon, could mean no good to her"—are left undeveloped. Were it not for the songs, the piece could scarcely exist.

But electing to write, Toomer was too canny to try to carry literature further into music than this. *Cane* is, from one point of view, the record of his search for suitable literary forms. We can see him seeking guidance and in several of the stories, notably "Fern" and "Avey," it is the hand of Sherwood Anderson that he takes hold. But Anderson leads toward formlessness and Toomer shakes him off for Waldo Frank in such pieces as "Theatre" where the design becomes clear and the parts are held in a vital esthetic union. Finally, he breaks through in a free dramatic form of his own, the play *Kabnis* which still awaits production by an American theatre that cries for good native drama and yet lacks the wit to perceive the talent of Toomer. ⟨. . .⟩

He is a dynamic symbol of what all artists of our time should be doing, if they are to command our trust. He has mastered his craft. Now he seeks a purpose that will convince him that his craft is nobly employed. Obviously, to his search there is no end, but in his search there is bound to occur a fusion of his experience, and it is this fused experience that will give profundity to his later work. His way is not the way of the minor art master, but the way of the major master of art. And that is why his potential literary significance outweighs the actualized literary significance of so many of his contemporaries.

> Gorham B. Munson, "The Significance of Jean Toomer," *Opportunity* 3, No. 3 (September 1925): 262–63

JEAN TOOMER   In my writing I was working, at various times, on all the main forms. Essays, articles, poems, short stories, reviews, and a long piece somewhere between a novel and a play. Before I had even so much as glimpsed the possibility of writing *Cane*, I had written a trunk full of manuscripts. The phrase "trunk full" is often used loosely. I mean it literally and exactly. But what difficulties I had! I had in me so much experience so twisted up that not a thing would come out until by sheer force I had dragged it forth. Only now and again did I experience spontaneous writing.

Most of it was will and sweat. And nothing satisfied me. Not a thing had I done which I thought merited publication—or even sending to a magazine. I wrote and wrote and put each thing aside, regarding it as simply one of the exercises of my apprenticeship. Often I would be depressed and almost despair over the written thing. But, on the other hand, I became more and more convinced that I had the real stuff in me. And slowly but surely I began getting the "feeling" of my medium, a sense of form, of words, of sentences, rhythms, cadences, and rhythmic patterns. And then, after several years work, suddenly, it was as if a door opened and I knew without doubt that I was *inside. I knew literature!* And what was my joy!

But many things happened before that time came! ⟨. . .⟩

I came in contact with an entirely new body of ideas. Buddhist philosophy, the Eastern teachings, occultism, theosophy. Much of the writing itself seemed to me to be poorly done; and I was certain that the majority of the authors of these books had only third or fourth-rate minds, or less. But I extracted the ideas from their settings, and they seemed to me among the most extraordinary I had ever heard. It is natural to me to put my whole heart into anything that really interests me—as long as I am interested. For the time being, only that thing exists in the world. These ideas challenged and stimulated me. Despite my literary purpose, I was compelled to know something more about them. So, for a time, I turned my back on literature and plunged into this kind of reading. I read far and wide, for more than eight months. Then, I became dissatisfied with just reading. I wanted to do some of the things they suggested. I wanted to see some of the things with my own eyes. I myself wanted a personal all-around experience of the world these books seemed to open. I tried several of the exercises; but then, abruptly stopped them. I concluded they were not for me. In general, I concluded that all of that was not for me. I was in this physical, tangible, earthly world, and I knew little enough of it. It was the part of wisdom to learn more and to be able to do more in this, before I began exploring and adventuring into other worlds. So I came back to earth and to literature. But I had profited in many ways by my excursion. The Eastern World, the ancient scriptures had been brought to my notice. Also, our own Christian Bible. I had read it as if it were a new book. Just simply as a work of literature I was convinced that we had nothing to equal it. Not even Shakespeare— my old God—wrote language of such grand perfection. And my religious nature, given a cruel blow by Clarence Darrow and naturalism and atheism, but not, as I found, destroyed by them—my religious nature which had been sleeping was vigorously aroused. ⟨. . .⟩

Once during this period I read many books on the matter of race and the race problem in America. Rarely had I encountered the nonsense contained in most of these books. It was evident to me, who had seen both the white and the colored worlds, and both from the inside, that the authors of these writings had little or no experience of the matters they were dealing with. Their pages showed very little more than strings of words expressive of personal prejudices and preferences. I felt that I should write on this matter. I did write several fragments of essays. And I did a lot of thinking. Among other things, I again worked over my own position, and formulated it with more fullness and exactitude. I wrote a poem called, "The First American," the idea of which is, that here in America we are in the process of forming a new race, that I was one of the first conscious members of this race.

> Jean Toomer, "The Cane Years" (c. 1932), *The Wayward and the Seeking: A Collection of Writings by Jean Toomer*, ed. Darwin T. Turner (Washington, DC: Howard University Press, 1980), pp. 117–21

STERLING BROWN   Jean Toomer is best as a poet in the beautiful prose of *Cane* (1923). His few poems in the same volume, however, are original and striking. Jean Toomer has written that Georgia opened him up; "Reapers" and "Cotton Song" show this awaking to folk material. In "Georgia Dusk" there is a sense of the ominous mystery of the Southland:

> The sawmill blows its whistle, buzz-saws stop,
> And silence breaks the bud of knoll and hill . . .,
> Smoke from the pyramidal sawdust pile
> Curls up, blue ghosts of trees. . . .
> . . . the chorus of the cane
> Is caroling a vesper to the stars. . . .

With a mastery of the best rhythmical devices of Negro folk-music, "Song of the Son" expresses the return of the younger Negro to a consciousness of identity with his own, a return to folk sources, to the "caroling softly souls of slavery"—

> O land and soil, red soil and sweet-gum tree,
> So scant of grass, so profligate of pines,

> Now just before an epoch's sun declines,
> Thy son, in time, I have returned to thee,
> Thy son, I have in time returned to thee.
> In time, for though the sun is setting on
> A song-lit race of slaves, it has not set. . . .

In spite of the small number of his poems, Toomer remains one of the finest and most influential of Negro poets. His long silence has been broken with the publication of "Blue Meridian," a rather long poem calling for a "new America, to be spiritualized by each new American." In it there are only occasional references to Negro life:

> The great African races sent a single wave
> And singing riplets to sorrow in red fields
> Sing a swan song, to break rocks
> And immortalize a hiding water-boy. . . .

Sterling Brown, *Negro Poetry and Drama* (Washington, DC: Associates in Negro Folk Education, 1937), pp. 67–68

J. SAUNDERS REDDING   *Cane* was experimental, a potpourri of poetry and prose, in which the latter element is significant because of the influence it had on the course of Negro fiction. Mr. Toomer is indebted to Sherwood Anderson and Waldo Frank for much in his prose style, but his material is decidedly his own. Sometimes he falls short of his best abilities for lack of government, as in the story "Kabnis," which says and does much but obscures much more. Sometimes he succeeds splendidly, as in the sketches "Carma" and "Fern," in which feeling and language are restrained and genuine. But often he wallows in feeling and grows inarticulate with a rush of words.

Though *Cane* was in the nature of an experiment (the conclusion to which we are fearful of never knowing, for since 1923 Toomer has published practically nothing) it established the precedent of self-revelation that has characterized the writings of Negroes on all levels ever since. At first completely absorbed in fulfilling his opportunity for release, the new Negro had no time for new forms. In his anxiety and relief he did not reflect that he was pouring new wine into old bottles. In truth, he was somewhat distrustful of his new place in the sun. He was afraid of being a fad, the momentary focus of the curiosity of dilettantes, charlatans, and student sociologists. It was common sense for him to attempt to establish himself on something more solid than the threatrical reputation of Florence Mills or the *bizarreries* of what many people thought to be the Greenwich Village influence. New forms were faddish froth: material the marrow. And what more arresting material than the self-revealing truth!

> J. Saunders Redding, *To Make a Poet Black* (Chapel Hill: University of North Carolina Press, 1939), pp. 105–6

ROBERT BONE   In spite of his wide and perhaps primary association with white intellectuals, as an artist Toomer never underestimated the importance of his Negro identity. He attained a universal vision not by ignoring race as a local truth, but by coming face to face with his particular tradition. His pilgrimage to Georgia was a conscious attempt to make contact with his hereditary roots in the Southland. Of Georgia, Toomer wrote: "There one finds soil in the sense that the Russians know it—the soil every art and literature that is to live must be embedded in." This scene of soil is central to *Cane* and to Toomer's artistic vision. "When one is on the soil of one's ancestors," his narrator remarks, "most anything can come to one."

What comes to Toomer, in the first section of *Cane*, is a vision of the parting soul of slavery:

> . . . for though the sun is setting on
> A song-lit race of slaves, it has not set;
> Though late, O soil, it is not too late yet
> To catch thy plaintive soul, leaving, soon gone.

The soul of slavery persists in the "supper-getting-ready songs" of the black women who live on the Dixie Pike—a road which "has grown from a goat path in Africa." It persists in "the soft, listless cadence of Georgia's South," in the hovering spirit of a comforting Jesus, and in the sudden violence of the Georgia moon. It persists above all in the people, white and black, who have become Andersonian "grotesques" by virtue of their slave inheritance. Part I of *Cane* is in fact a kind of Southern *Winesburg, Ohio*. It consists of the portraits of six women—all primitives—in which an Andersonian narrator mediates between the reader and the author's vision of life on the Dixie Pike.

> Robert Bone, *The Negro Novel in America* (New Haven: Yale University Press, 1958), pp. 81–82

DARWIN T. TURNER   The actual beginning of Jean Toomer, writer, probably can be dated from ⟨. . .⟩ the spring of 1920. While chasing many gleams, he had read extensively in atheism, naturalism, socialism, sociology, psychology, and the dramas of Shaw. To these scientific, philosophical, and social writings, he had added *Wilhelm Meister* of Goethe, the romances of Victor Hugo, and the verse of Walt Whitman. After his abortive crusade in the shipyard, he had reaccepted capitalism as a necessary evil. Dismayed because his atheism had shocked a Quaker girl, he had reaffirmed his faith in God and in religion, even though he refused to believe in orthodox creeds and churches. Introduced now to a literary world of such people as Lola Ridge, Edwin Arlington Robinson, and Waldo Frank, he was dazzled with the prospect of retiring from arid philosophies into a cultural aristocracy.

Looking back from a diary written in 1930, he saw the Toomer of the early twenties as a vanity-burdened poseur who adopted the manners of a poet, a poet's appearance, and a French-sounding name—Jean. A more objective observer sees a seriously confused young man of twenty-five, who was not content to be average, but who had discovered nothing at which to be great; who wanted to guide, to instruct, to lead, to dominate, but who would withdraw completely if he could not; and who habitually discontinued studies with startling abruptness, not because he had mastered them, but because he had lost interest or, as with music, had decided that he could not become a master. This, however, was the tortured soul hidden by the ever present mask of intellect, confidence, and charm which caused Waldo Frank to write, "You are one of those men one must see but once to know the timbre and the truth of."

Darwin T. Turner, "Jean Toomer: Exile," *In a Minor Chord: Three Afro-American Writers and Their Search for Identity* (Carbondale: Southern Illinois University Press, 1971), pp. 10–11

JEAN WAGNER   "Blue Meridian" is beyond a doubt the concluding step in a long process of meditation, for its central idea is already contained in embryo in an essay published seven years earlier and entitled "Race Problems and Modern Society."

In this essay, Toomer begins by noting "the changes of forms and of modes" that had occurred at a constantly accelerated pace during his own lifetime: "The principles of cohesion and crystallization are being rapidly withdrawn from the materials of old forms, with a consequent break up of these forms, a setting free of these materials, with the possibility that the principles of cohesion and crystallization will recombine the stuff of life and make new forms." These cataclysms affect not only the material features of man's life but also the actual forms of relationships between men.

Alongside this development there is, contrariwise, a strengthening of some other forms of modern society which, remaining exempt from the dissolution noted above, even tend to expand and establish themselves more firmly. In particular these are, according to Toomer, the Western world's economic, political, legal, and military concepts, which dig themselves in and work against the evolutionary forces.

He proceeds by placing, within the context of these related yet hostile movements, the racial problems, especially those of the United States, which cannot be considered apart from the other principal forms of the social order. Here the effect of the evolutionary factors is to bring about an ever closer resemblance between such Negro social types as the businessman, politician, educator, student, writer, etc., and the corresponding white types. Yet, on the other hand, whites and blacks shut themselves up ever more tightly in their separatism with the consequence, for example, that interracial marriage becomes no less heinous in the eyes of blacks than of whites.

Given this crystallization of the race question, Toomer is led to advocate, as a way out of the impasse, "a selective fusion of the racial and cultural factors of America, in order that the best possible stock and culture may be produced."

Though the line of argument in this essay is buttressed by scientific considerations, Toomer's thinking is essentially that of a poet and humanist. We are, in any case, under no obligation to pass judgment on the feasibility of the plan, which concerns us only insofar as it may serve to throw light on the genesis of "Blue Meridian."

Race, in this poem, acquires a totally different dimension from what we encountered in Cane. As in the essay discussed above, it takes place in the much vaster setting of the "Myth of America," to adopt Hart Crane's expression. For is not America indeed, as Walt Whitman declared it, "the race of races" and also "the greatest poem"? "Blue Meridian" quite certainly owes something to The Bridge, but both alike are indebted to Whitman and, through him, to the American tradition born with the Pilgrim Fathers, according to which the New World must necessarily be new, in the most literal sense of the word.

The fundamental thesis of "Blue Meridian" is the need for a regenerated America, to be achieved through the regeneration of each individual and each community composing it, of an America once more united around the spiritual dream of its founders.

> It is a new America,
> To be spiritualized by each new American.

What must be found once more is the whole man in his primordial unity, whether this is brought about by the collective effort of millions of men or attained by an elite of apostles ("twelve men") among whom, as Toomer saw things, one would have to place poets:

> Lift, lift thou walking forces!
> Let us feel the energy of animals,
> The energy of rumps and bull-bent heads
> Crashing the barrier to man.
> It must spiral on!
> A million men, or twelve men,
> Must crash the barrier to the next higher form.

Jean Wagner, *Black Poets of the United States: From Paul Lawrence Dunbar to Langston Hughes*, tr. Kenneth Douglas (Urbana: University of Illinois Press, 1973), pp. 272–74

RICHARD ELDRIDGE   While the poetic quality of Toomer's prose is in many respects bolder and more successful than much of his poetry, the poems nevertheless are an essential part of his "song." As in his prose, many of his poems are dusk songs, reflecting not only the mood of the land but also the sense of the people. "Nullo" is a poem which shows the deep connection between earth and sky at a time of day when limits are hard to define and therefore blend with the limitless:

> A spray of pine-needles,
> Dipped in western horizon gold,
> Fell onto a path.
> Dry moulds of cow-hoofs.
> In the forest.
> Rabbits knew not of their falling,
> Nor did the forest catch aflame.

The poem places before the reader the merest glimpse of a moment when a spectacle occurs without notice but for the poet: the sun setting fire to the edges of a spray of pine-needles as it falls to the ground. The visual impression is precise; not only are we shown the path, but the shapes in the path, "Dry moulds of cow-hoofs." The silence of such an eventful non-event protects it from all but the poet's eye: "Rabbits knew not of their falling, / Nor did the forest catch aflame." The pine spray catches the fire yet does not spread it beyond the spray's own beauty. The cows have parted until the next day, and the rabbits are unconscious of the passing. Such is the attraction of sunset, when the poet's eye can make the seemingly insignificant moment into a significant statement.

As in the sadness of Karintha's waste, Toomer's dusk poems often are commentaries on the sadness of a dying culture. "Song of the Son" has correctly been singled out as embodying the central idea of Toomer's Southern experience. In the poem, dusk is connected most clearly with Toomer's thesis of the "swan-song" of the black folk heritage. The poem's message is that the narrator, ostensibly Toomer, has returned to his Southern roots in time to record the rural life in art which will outlast the black man. A letter to Waldo Frank clarifies the point of view with which Toomer wrote the poem:

> There is one thing about the Negro in America which most
> thoughtful persons seem to ignore: the Negro is in solution, in the
> process of solution. As an entity, the race is loosing [sic] its body,
> and its soul is approaching a common soul. If one holds his eye to
> individuals and sections, race is starkly evident, and racial
> continuity seems assured. One is even led to believe that the
> thing we call Negro beauty will always be attributable to a clearly
> defined physical source. But the fact is, that if anything comes up
> now, pure Negro, it will be a swan-song. The negro [sic] of the
> folk-song has all but passed away: the Negro of the emotional
> church is fading. A hundred years from now these Negroes, if they
> exist at all will live in art. . . . The supreme fact of mechanical
> civilization is that you become part of it, or get sloughed off
> (under). Negroes have no culture to resist it with (and if they
> had, their position would be identical to that of the Indians),
> hence industrialism the more readily transforms them. A few
> generations from now, the Negro will still be dark, and a portion
> of his psychology will spring from this fact, but in all else he will
> be a conformist to the general outlines of American civilization,
> or of American chaos. In my own stuff, in those pieces that come

> closest to the old Negro, to the spirit saturated with folk-song:
> Karintha and Fern, the dominant emotion is sadness derived from
> a sense of fading, from a knowledge of my futility to check
> solution. There is nothing about these pieces of the bouyant [sic]
> expression of new race. The folk-songs themselves are of the same
> order. The deepest of them: "I ain't got long to stay here."

If the expression of folk-roots is to be recorded in art, what better way to
record it than by creating a pattern of song to drift from story to story,
poem to poem, usually at dusk when toil and need are reflected upon with
a soul-response? If the culture is dying, what better moment to frame that
death than the moment of day which heightens life by the very imminence
of darkness and, symbolically, death?

> Richard Eldridge, "The Unifying Images in Part One of Jean Toomer's *Cane*," CLA
> *Journal* 12, No. 3 (March 1979): 194–96

NELLIE Y. McKAY   *Balo* and *Natalie Mann* are products of the brief
time during which Toomer had the desire to add the unique richness of
the Afro-American experience to American literature. ⟨. . .⟩

Balo and *Natalie Mann* are two very different plays, and in them Toomer
explores two distinctly separate forms of dramatic techniques. The first is
a one-act folk play, the second, a full-length experiment in expressionist
theater. In *Balo*, the southern setting, the single-day action, and the poor,
rural, close-to-the-earth and very religious characters contrast sharply with
the living rooms of the Washington, D.C., middle class, the cabarets of the
counterculture, the year-long action, and the affluent, urbane, and upwardly
mobile characters who make "refined" culture their religion, who engage
in endless conversations about the definition of art and whom we meet in
Natalie Mann. In these plays, the differences in basic values between these
two groups of people—a result of the development of class differences among
black people between the end of the Civil War and 1920—becomes clear
as Toomer describes folk culture and regionalism in one and the black need
for erudition and cosmopolitanism in the other. ⟨. . .⟩

The differences between *Balo* and *Natalie Mann* make it clear that
although Toomer was critical of some of the realities of black folk life, its
good qualities made a positive impression on his imagination, whereas there
was little he could recommend in the culture of middle-class America, the

negative aspects of which he wanted to expose. From an emotional and philosophical standpoint, Toomer looked back to the African/American folk culture, identified himself with what he found spiritually uplifting in it, and made it a source of artistic inspiration.

Nellie Y. McKay, *Jean Toomer, Artist: A Study of His Literary Life and Work 1894–1936* (Chapel Hill: University of North Carolina Press, 1984), pp. 60–61, 79

CHARLES T. DAVIS   The preoccupation with the problems of consciousness is responsible for the design of *Cane*. Toomer is not content simply to explore the situations in which an alien Northern intelligence confronts Southern realities; he is as much concerned with analyzing the factors that have shaped the Northern mind. He sees the necessity for regional connection, for the Northern black to acquire the emotional strengths that black Southerners still possess, though they may be rapidly losing them. What haunts Toomer's mind is a circle based upon regional relationships, or, more accurately a broken circle, since the author does not reach the point in *Cane* of successful prefiguration, the emancipation for the full existence for man, what would be called later the "all around development of man," involving the "constructive functioning" of body, emotions, and mind.

Toomer's own comments on the structure for *Cane* are invaluable and offer a beginning for any discussion of the organization of the whole work. In December 1922, Waldo Frank received a letter from Toomer announcing the completion of *Cane* and defining the principles which were intended to give unity to his achievement:

> From three angles, *Cane*'s design is a circle. Aesthetically, from simple forms to complex ones, and back to simple forms. Regionally, from the South up to the North, and back to the South again. Or, from the North down into the South, and then a return North. From the point of view of the spiritual entity behind the work, the curve really starts with Bona and Paul (awakening), plunges into Kabnis, emerges in Karintha, etc., swings upward into Theater and Box Seat, and ends (pauses) in Harvest Song.

Toomer's first comment on form is plain enough and requires little expla-nation. The Georgia tales and "Kabnis" are reasonably straightforward narratives, with intensities that are either lyric or dramatic. They are without the symbolic complexity of the middle section of *Cane*, the one devoted to the North. We find here the experimental sketches "Seventh Street," "Rhobert," and "Calling Jesus," presenting a level of abstraction not discovered elsewhere. ⟨. . .⟩

Cane owes everything to the symbolic representation of region and race. Toomer discovered his blackness in Georgia, and armed with this revelation he was able to construct a pattern of life which contrasted with what he had seen about him in the cities of the North. Neither pattern was to be satisfying finally. The writing of *Cane* occurred at a very special moment in Toomer's life. This time came when his awareness of his own heritage was heightened by the impending death of his grandfather Pinchback, when his sense of the corruption of modern urban society was keen as a result of a close intellectual association with Waldo Frank and Sherwood Anderson, and when the exposure to black rural life in Georgia resolved momentarily his own ambivalent and uncertain feelings about racial identity. This moment was enough to link him to other writers of the Harlem Renaissance, who were at the time struggling to conquer feelings of uncertainty and inadequacy of a different kind in an effort to achieve an expression of that which was most authentic in their lives.

> Charles T. Davis, "Jean Toomer and the South: Region and Race as Elements within a Literary Imagination," *The Harlem Renaissance Re-examined*, ed. Victor A. Kramer (New York: AMS Press, 1987), pp. 193, 197

CYNTHIA EARL KERMAN and RICHARD ELDRIDGE

⟨Toomer⟩ was not seeking a shift in a category attached to his own name, such as from black to white; he wished to be neither white nor black. The vision of the universal man was the benchmark of his identity, and perhaps he accurately perceived himself as the embodiment of the greater American soul, a concept that Waldo Frank and others continued to encourage. Toomer's appearance, he noted, caused people on separate occasions to think that he was of eleven different nationalities. As for biological forebears, he could not be sure but was probably somewhere between one-eighth and one-sixteenth black. And he had lived among blacks, among whites, among Jews, and in groups organized without racial labels around a shared interest such as literature or psychology, moving freely from any one of these groups to any other. One mark of membership in the "colored" group, he said, was acceptance of the "color line" with its attendant expectations; neither his family nor he had ever been so bound. To be in the white group would also imply the exclusion of the other.

> What then am I?
> I am at once no one of the races and I am all of them.
> I belong to no one of them and I belong to all.
> I am, in a strict racial sense, a member of a new race.

This new race of mixed people, now forming all over the world but especially in America, "may be the turning point for the return of mankind, now divided into hostile races, to one unified race, namely, to the human race." It was a new race, but also the oldest. The different racial and national groups could still contribute their distinctive richness: "I say to the colored group that, as a human being, I am one of them. . . . I say to the white group that, as a human being, I am one of them. As a white man, I am not one of them. . . . I am an American. As such, I invite them [both], not as [colored or] white people, but *as Americans*, to participate in whatever creative work I may be able to do."

Thus Toomer propounded the rather unpopular view that the racial issue in America would be resolved only when white America could accept the fact that its racial "purity" was a myth, that indeed its racial isolation produced blandness and lack of character. On the other hand, racial purity among blacks was just as much a myth and only encourages defensiveness and unconscious imitation, like that of an adolescent who defines his revolt against his parents by the very values he is trying to renounce. Race, he said, was a fictional construct, of no use for understanding people: "Human blood is human blood. Human beings are human beings. . . . No racial or social factors can adequately account for the uniqueness of each—or for the individual differences which people display concurrently with basic commonality."

Cynthia Earl Kerman and Richard Eldridge, *The Lives of Jean Toomer: A Hunger for Wholeness* (Baton Rouge: Louisiana State University Press, 1987), pp. 341–42

HOUSTON A. BAKER, JR.   The 1920s presented a problem for the writer who wished to give a full and honest representation of black American life; for him the traditional images, drawn from the authors of the Plantation Tradition and the works of Paul Laurence Dunbar, were passé. The contemporary images, captured in Carl Van Vechten's *Nigger Heaven* (1926) and Claude McKay's *Home to Harlem* (1928), were not designed to elucidate a complex human existence, for they were reflections of that search for the bizarre and the exotic that was destined to flourish in an age of raccoon coats, bathtub gin, and "wine-flushed, bold-eyed" whites who caught the A-train to Harlem and spent the evening slumming, or seeking some élan vital for a decadent but prosperous age. That only two small printings of *Cane* appeared during the 1920s is not striking: the miracle is that it was published at all. Toomer did not choose the approbation that a scintillating (if untrue) portrayal of the black man could bring in the twenties, nor did he speak sotto voce about the amazing progress the black man had made in American society and his imminent acceptance by a fond white world. *Cane* is a symbolically complex work that employs lyrical intensity and stream-of-consciousness narration to portray the journey of an artistic soul toward creative fulfillment; it is unsparing in its criticism of the inimical aspects of the black American heritage and resonant in its praise of the spiritual beauty to be discovered there. An examination of the journey toward genuine, liberating black art presented in *Cane* reveals Toomer as a writer of genius and the book itself as a protest novel, a portrait of the artist, and a thorough delineation of the black situation. These aspects of the work explain its signal place among the achievements of the Harlem Renaissance, and they help to clarify the reaction of a white reading public— a public nurtured on the minstrel tradition, the tracts of the new Negro, and the sensational antics of Carl Van Vechten's blacks—which allowed it to go out of print without a fair hearing.

> Houston A. Baker, Jr., "Journey toward Black Art: Jean Toomer's *Cane*," *Afro-American Poetics: Revisions of Harlem and the Black Aesthetic* (Madison: University of Wisconsin Press, 1988), pp. 17–19

ROBERT B. JONES   In the summer of 1938 Toomer moved to Bucks County, Pennsylvania, where he was almost immediately attracted to Quakerism. During his apprenticeship with the Society of Friends, he immersed himself in Quaker religious philosophy, wrote numerous essays on George Fox and Quakerism, and, in 1940, joined the Society of Friends. His interest in Quaker religious philosophy sprang from his own idea that the

Society of Friends provided a radical venture beyond ⟨Gurdjieff's⟩ Objective
Consciousness to a vital and transforming religious faith.

> Quakers assembled, I had been told, for silent worship and waited
> for the spirit to move them. This appealed to me because I had
> practiced meditation. Years before I had read a brief account of
> George Fox that impressed me. I had heard of the Quaker
> reputation for practicing what they preached . . . Prior to coming
> into contact with Friends I had been convinced that God is both
> immanent and transcendent, and that the purpose of life is to
> grow up to God; that within man there is a wonderful power that
> can transform him, lift him into new birth; that we have it in us
> to rise to a life wherein brotherhood is manifest and war
> impossible.

To define the poetry of this period as Christian Existential, two factors
must be considered. In the first place, Toomer envisioned Quaker religious
philosophy as a bridge between two (Kierkegaardian) levels of consciousness,
the ethical or social concerns of Objective Consciousness, and the religious
or theistic concerns of Christianity. Indeed, in 1938 he sought to reconcile
Gurdjieffian idealism with Quakerism by organizing a cooperative of both
Quakers and lay individuals called Friends of Being. ⟨. . .⟩ the ostensible
conflict remains as the basis for a pervasive Christian Existentialism. In the
second place, Quakerism and Christian Existentialism comprise fundamen-
tally the same religious philosophy, both in contrast to Gurdjieffian idealism.
Thus in temperament and philosophy, Toomer's consciousness is best
described as Christian Existential. And it is precisely this consciousness
which is the genesis of his spiritual odyssey as a Quaker poet.

Robert B. Jones, "Introduction," *The Collected Poems of Jean Toomer*, ed. Robert B.
Jones (Chapel Hill: University of North Carolina Press, 1988), pp. xxv–xxvi

---

RUDOLPH P. BYRD   Of Toomer's several plays, *The Sacred Factory*
is plainly the most important because he achieved within this expressionist,
four-act drama a balance between his goals as a promoter of the Gurdjieff
system and his responsibilities as a dramatist. The Gurdjieffian elements
emerge as organic parts of Toomer's drama. We are interested in the conflict
between John and Mary because Toomer created a situation that inspires
empathy. We are interested in the function and power of the Being because

Toomer created a situation that is compelling and dramatic. In this particular work, the theories of the Gurdjieff system extend and amplify Toomer's concerns and preoccupations as a dramatist. They increase the depth and range of meaning. Toomer did not make the mistake, as he did in "A Drama of the Southwest" and "Pilgrims, Did You Say?" of burdening the work with the technical, specialized terminology of the Gurdjieff system. *The Sacred Factory* is devoid of Gurdjieffian cant, banter, and undisguised propaganda. Action and dialogue rise unfettered, unencumbered, to the level of meaning and ritual.

Like *Balo* and "Kabnis," *The Sacred Factory* is a drama deserving production and scholarly study. In these works, the poet of *Cane* demonstrated his potential and ability as a dramatist. We do not find in these plays, as we do in many of the others, the awkward musings of an amateur dramatist or the extremely confident, faintly patronizing pronouncements of a Gurdjieffian devotee. Instead we find dramatizations of what might be termed the three stages of Toomer's own quest for wholeness, for an "intelligible scheme." These three stages—meditation, search, and discovery—are subtexts within larger texts that possess abiding relevance and profound implications for our own spiritual odyssey.

Rudolph P. Byrd, *Jean Toomer's Years with Gurdjieff: Portrait of an Artist 1923–1936* (Athens: University of Georgia Press, 1990), p. 179

CHARLES R. LARSON   Toomer was raised as a white person. Sociologically and culturally that is what he considered himself to be until the 1909 conversation with his grandfather, when P. B. S. informed him that Eliza Stewart may have been of mixed heritage. Until that moment, he had apparently never seriously considered the possibility, though the effect of this knowledge so traumatized him that he altered it and called himself an American. There were the years following Nina Toomer Coombs's death, when Jean and his grandparents lived in a racially mixed neighborhood and he attended a predominantly black school. But as soon as he graduated from high school, he made a hasty withdrawal from this first foray into black life and skittered off to Wisconsin. His autobiographical writings make the significance of that location absolutely clear: if he continued to live in a racially mixed community, people might begin to regard him as a Negro. ⟨. . .⟩

Toomer's connection to and with Harlem Renaissance might best be called an accident of time and place. If he had not told Waldo Frank and others that he was P. B. S. Pinchback's grandson, he might never have been connected with the Renaissance. If he had not used Waldo Frank's friendship and influence among New York publishers—blatantly, to his own advantage, it should be said—he might have remained unpublished. More likely, he would have found a publisher who would not have tried to promote him as a black writer, and today he would simply be regarded as another American author (like Waldo Frank, Sherwood Anderson, or even William Faulkner) who chose to write about black life in the United States. Clearly, by the time *Cane* saw print, Toomer deeply regretted being classified as a Negro author.

To his surprise and horror, the classification stuck. Why wouldn't it? *Cane* is one of the masterpieces of twentieth-century American fiction. Though its mixed form is often initially confusing, the statement it makes about ethnic pride through the nourishment of one's roots is absolutely indisputable. On a personal level, *Cane* is not simply about Jean Toomer's inability to accept his blackness but about America's failure to accept its Africanness. Still, people of differing ethnic origins have been proud to claim the novel, as if proprietary rights are a guarantee of artistic greatness. Fortunately, the work can stand on its own creative merit, with or without the ethnic claimants. Like *Huckleberry Finn* and *Light in August* and *Invisible Man*, Toomer's novel addresses one of the major issues of American life— racism in the United States. It is very much a social document about that specific American malady, yet its affirmation of blackness is never weighted down by the romantic sentiment of some of Toomer's contemporaries' work.

Instead, one might say that *Cane* catalogues the frustrations and psychoses of black life in a kleptomaniacal world, where one culture steals from another while simultaneously beating it down. In the jealousy that binds the two cultures together, Toomer discovers not only life and heritage but also poetry. *Cane* was Toomer's ultimate homage to black life, his praise song of a way of life he himself was unable to embrace.

Charles R. Larson, *Invisible Darkness: Jean Toomer and Nella Larsen* (Iowa City: University of Iowa Press, 1993), pp. 201–2

▧ *Bibliography*

Cane. 1923.

Essentials. 1931.

The Flavor of Man. 1949.

The Wayward and the Seeking: A Collection of Writings. Ed. Darwin T. Turner.
    1980.

Collected Poems. Ed. Robert B. Jones. 1988.

Frank Wilson
1886–1956

FRANCIS H. WILSON was born in Harlem, New York, in 1886, although 1891 is often given as his birth date. Little information exists on his childhood, but his involvement in vaudeville theatre began early on, and in 1908 he organized a vaudeville troupe, the Carolina Comedy Four. He experienced some success as an actor and baritone singer, but quit the troupe in 1911 to become a mail carrier. Wilson viewed this job primarily as an opportunity to tour Harlem and observe its residents in order to obtain material for plays. Between 1914 and 1916, Wilson wrote prolifically for the Anita Bush Players, supposedly writing a playlet every six to eight weeks for a period of three years (unfortunately, all his material from this period remains unpublished). In 1916 the Anita Bush Players moved from the Lincoln Theater to the Lafayette Theater and became the Lafayette Players, and Wilson moved with them, making his first non-vaudeville stage appearance in the 1917 production of a play entitled *Deep Purple*.

After World War I Wilson studied acting at the American Academy of Dramatic Art and joined the Provincetown Players as a supporting actor. His career as a successful professional actor extended almost thirty years; some of his notable roles included supporting roles in Eugene O'Neill's *All God's Chillun Got Wings* and *The Emperor Jones*, as well as a leading role in *In Abraham's Bosom* and the title role in DuBose Heyward's *Porgy*, which later became the musical *Porgy and Bess*. Wilson also played in the 1936 film version of *The Emperor Jones*, as well as the film version of *Green Pastures* and *Watch on the Rhine*, but quit film acting in protest over the stereotyped roles available to black actors.

In 1920 Wilson won first place for drama in the *Opportunity* Contest Awards with *Sugar Cain* (republished in 1927 as *Sugar Cane*), a drama about a black woman raped by a white man in the Deep South. Although *Sugar Cain* was slated for Broadway, that production never occurred, and *Sugar Cain* was performed in Harlem instead. Wilson's next significant hit was *Meek Mose* (1928), which was the first play to be produced on Broadway by a black producer; it had a moderately successful run. It was revived by the Works Progress Administration in 1934 as *Brother Mose* and published in mimeograph by the U.S. National Service Bureau in 1937. Wilson's next play, *The Wall Between* (1929), was also slated for a Broadway production but never produced.

In 1936 Wilson's drama of racial solidarity, *Walk Together Chillun*, became the New York Federal Theatre Project's first sizeable production. Although it only ran for nineteen performances, more than 10,000 people saw the play. After 1936 Wilson wrote scenarios for three movies, *Paradise in Harlem* (1939), *Murder on Lenox Avenue* (1941), and *Sunday Sinners* (1941), all produced by Jack Goldberg. Wilson retired from theatre in 1955 and died on February 16, 1956, in Jamaica, New York, shortly after a severe stroke. He was survived by his wife, Effie King Wilson (formerly of Bert Williams and George Walker's theatrical troupe), his son Emmett Barrymore Wilson, and his two stepchildren, Marguerite Wilson and Monte T. Ray.

▨ *Critical Extracts*

J. BROOKS ATKINSON   In *Meek Mose* the majority of the characters do not seem to be real people, not as real as those in *Porgy* or *Goat Alley*, but exaggerations of real people. And when put into such a play as *Meek Mose* that play becomes no more a reflection of negroes or negro problems than *Turn to the Right* was a reflection of American farming conditions.

On the other hand, the point may well be brought up that *Meek Mose* is not supposed to be a realistic portrayal of negroes or of contemporary negro problems, but simply a theatrical entertainment. In this case the opinion that such a theatre should locate in Harlem, where it would be of most service, might be in order.

Among the assets of last night's production were some spirituals, effectively intoned at all the high points in the action, and one or two fairly straight performances, notably those of J. Lawrence Criner and Charles H. Moore. The latter played Mose, an inevitable turner of the other cheek, who suffers patiently through an assemblage of woes to triumph in the end when oil is found on his property. ⟨. . .⟩

Mayor Walker was introduced to the audience by Ferdinand Q. Morton, a Civil Service Commissioner, who is interested in the movement to establish a negro repertory company.

"This is a city where men are measured by their achievements," the Mayor said, speaking from the stage. "This play tonight is an indication of the progress of the negro group in our city. After all, no matter what the veneer is, the best we can do is just to be human. And this is a vindication of the progress of American Government."

J. Brooks Atkinson, "Mayor at Opening of Negro Theatre," *New York Times*, 7 February 1928, p. 30

UNSIGNED   *Meek Mose*, a comedy drama of Negro life written by a Negro and played by Negro actors, opened its first night at the Princess Theatre, Thirty-ninth street near Broadway, Monday night. ⟨. . .⟩

The play is built around the beatitude, "The meek shall inherit the earth," and the dramatic crises hinge upon this premise. The modern and opposite belief in this idea clashes with the Negro's passivity as exemplified in Meek Mose Johnson, who believes all of his Bible and in waiting upon the Lord.

The scenes are laid in Mexia, Texas, where the white folks have shunted the Negroes from one location to another almost without protest. The majority of them decide to remain and fight it out, but put the matter up to Mose, the oldest and most respected resident.

Mose yields to the will of the white folks. They move to the "gut" and are ravaged by disease and discomfort and they blame Mose and make an attempt upon his life.

Through the efforts of Mr. Harmon, a white friend of Mose, oil is discovered in the "gut" and Mose and his neighbors become rich, thus proving, at least geographically, that the meek do inherit the earth.

The acting is excellent throughout, although a few rough spots must disappear as the play gets under way. ⟨. . .⟩

J. Lawrence Criner correctly typified the modern fighting spirit of the Negro in his clever characterization of Nathan, a young Negro who feared nobody, not even the white folks.

The supporting actors dovetailed their work with the main characters in a fine manner and the whole performance was really worth having the Mayor come out to see it.

The story, however, lacks sufficient depth, we think, to bring us to the theatre for the second time. We hope that it will have a liberal run, but we doubt it. It is, however, a very important step in the right direction.

Unsigned, "*Meek Mose* at The Princess," *New York Amsterdam News*, 8 February 1928, p. 9

FRANK WILSON   Just a few words regarding the Negro in the theatre—past, present and future. In the event that I digress, grow sentimental or you fail to agree with me, tolerance is the watchword. Are you listenin'? Let us go back. The cry today is: What is wrong with the theatre? Or what is wrong with the Negro in the theatre? Who knows?

I shall merely give my impressions of the theatre as it strikes me now, and what I think of the future. Years ago when I had witnessed a performance of Cole and Johnson's *Trip to Coontown* with Billy B. Johnson, and not Rosamond, at the old Star Theatre in 13th street and Broadway and also after watching a performance of Ward and Vokes in *The Head-Waiters* at the old Grand Opera House I raised my hand to high heaven and swore to the gods, or whoever else was listening, that I was going to be an actor, and a good one. Since that day I've been called dumb, overrated and weak, but the same ambition is with me, and I am carrying on.

In those days I never heard of the Negro doing anything in the drama in the theatre. He danced and he sang. If you went to a manager and told him you were an actor he'd immediately take you into a back room, point at the floor and tell you: Go ahead. Act. That was your cue to go into your dance. ⟨. . .⟩

These days no doubt are tough for the actor, but they are fine for the public. A play really has to be good to stand up today: and a Negro play has to be better than good. The greatest thing we have to combat is the effort of the producer to make us act and do things which we know to be entirely wrong so as to fit into his idea of what he thinks is "box office" or the pattern expected of us by the public. After all, we've been Negroes longer than any white man, and the wise director gives the Negro in the theatre free rein and lets him do things as a Negro would do them. And, naturally, gets good results.

Reuman Mamoulian did it in *Porgy* and I'm quite sure Marc Connelly did it in *Green Pastures*.

Things are bad in the theatre, as elsewhere, and the Negro in the theatre must suffer to an extent with the rest. He has this in his favor: he is fresh and new. He has untapped resources which when turned into the right channels can lift the American theatre out of the old beaten path, give it new life, and make it live again better than ever. This will take a love of theatre in us and, above all things, a desire to think differently and to try new things, also to experiment and get away from the old things of years ago because they were good then.

A few weeks ago I saw a dance at the Lafayette Theatre by Paul Meeres and a group of girls called "Frankenstein." It was marvelous. This new idea so astounded me that when I left the theatre I was walking on air, so to speak. Here was a Negro in the theatre trying something new. It was like a breath of fresh air. The Negro in the theatre today should be not discouraged, as this is his day.

People want new things, and where else can they get them but from those of us who can sing in the darkness, laugh at trouble and enjoy life as we live, whether we have a feast or a famine? No white man can do this. We've been acting somewhat, as a race, all out lives: we had to act or possibly we would have gone the way of the Indian.

Personally, I feel that the young boy or girl of my race in the theatre today is blessed. He is accepted as an actor or actress. In my day he was only expected to sing or dance, and not permitted to do anything else. The future looks great to me for the Negro in the theatre. Maybe I'm too optimistic, but my faith in this race of mine and the theatre will not permit me to think otherwise.

Frank Wilson, "The Theatre, Past and Present," *New York Amsterdam News*, 15 June 1932, p. 7

BROOKS ATKINSON   After displaying patience enough to make Job feel envious, the New York Federal Theatre Project raised the curtain on its first legitimate production last evening, *Walk Together Chillun*, which was acted at the Lafayette Theatre in Harlem. Theatregoers who remember Frank Wilson's acting in *In Abraham's Bosom* and *Porgy* probably know the sort of play he would instinctively write. It is simple, direct, and sincere. It is also frankly addressed to Negro audiences.

According to Broadway standards it is artless and sometimes unintelligible, for the narrative makes one or two transitions that are thoroughly confusing. WPA informers scattered through the first-night audience confided to this correspondent that the middle act had been discarded at the last moment. No doubt that accounts for the obvious break in the story in the center of the play.

But Mr. Wilson is urging the members of the colored race to patch up their sectional differences and to stand united in a fight for racial integrity. Setting his play in an unnamed city in the North, he shows how an infusion of Negroes from Georgia makes trouble and precipitates a race riot. The Georgia Negroes are imported by white contractors as cheap labor. They dislike the Northern Negroes who, in return, resent the competition of Negroes from the South. The result is a fracas over Negro politics which stirs up the whole town. When the Negroes are in trouble their sectional differences lose importance. When the whites are aroused they draw no distinctions. *Walk Together Chillun* concludes with an impassioned appeal for racial solidarity in the face of white hostility.

If the Federal regulators are looking for innocuous plays to employ the actors on WPA relief, they will have to avert their eyes from Mr. Wilson's jeremiad. He is no street-corner minstrel, strumming his lyre for Harlem tap-dancers. He is a crusader, and the laughs and roars his lines draw from the audience show that he knows where the sore points lie.

Following the familiar pattern for Negro plays, he includes one scene in a church where one or two spirituals are sung, and a dance hall scene where the mass revelry is solid with animal magnetism. Incidentally, that is a sound scheme for employing a large number of actors. But what the audience enjoyed most last evening were the attacks upon the duplicity of the whites, the complacence of the colored clergy and the cultivated manners of Negro leaders in the North. Although *Walk Together Chillun* is a patchwork play according to Broadway standards, there is obviously more to it than any white man is likely to understand. Mr. Wilson is talking to his comrades. He is not appealing for Times Square applause.

> Brooks Atkinson, "Opening of the WPA Drama in Harlem," *New York Times*, 5 February 1936, p. 15

FREDERICK W. BOND   In 1920, Frank Wilson, a postal clerk, wrote his *Sugar Cane*. This drama, while it was not pretentious, was superior to many of the plays written during the period. Wilson laid the scene of *Sugar Cane* in a modest home of contemporary Georgia. The circumstances surrounding the story deal with Paul, his wife, and their daughter, the last of whose actions create in the parents a bit of unpleasant suspicion. Within a period of three months, they become definitely aware of the fact that their daughter, Martha, has been violated. Martha names a young colored man, Howard Hill, who stayed with the family when he was home from the North on a short visit.

All hearts go out in sympathy for Martha when she, in a sense of shame and remorse, leaves home. Meanwhile, Fred, a son, voices certain suspicions to his parents concerning the movements of Lee Drayton, a white man who lives near by. Despite the fact that still further gossip had reached his ears, the father has such implicit confidence in white people that he does not, for a second, suppose that Lee Drayton, of all people, would seduce his daughter, and what is more he does not take kindly to Fred's accusation. Notwithstanding the fact that the finger of suspicion unmistakably points to the white man, the father swears vengeance against Howard Hill, declaring that he will kill the colored youth on sight. That, however, Martha's father fails to do, because she soon bears the child. Its appearance shows that it is, in reality, the child of a white man.

In 1928, Frank Wilson, who was also starring at the time in *Porgy*, actually captivated Broadway audiences with his *Meek Mose* which had its premiere at the Princess Theatre, January 23, 1928.

Docile Mose is supposed to be a patriarch among the better colored citizens of a Texas community. On the other hand, among the lower class he is referred to as a "church nigger of the white folks type," who relies upon the strength derived from Biblical quotations for his economic and social salvation. "Blessed are the meek, for they shall inherit the earth," Mose reminds the neighbors, one of whom disdainfully tells him that "he is full of rabbits." The whites admit that he is partly right, in that the Mighty Meek will inherit the earth. When the landlords evict him and his companions from the shacks, he advises his followers that the Lord will provide. Toward the end of the piece when disease and famine befall them, the group attempt to murder their leader because he appears to be a false prophet. As conditions become worse for old Mose, and the scripture fails to support him, oil is suddenly discovered on his land; whereupon, the entire community rejoices with spirituals, which furnish the production with its most satisfying bit of relief.

Wilson's characterization of the cynical wife of the hero has been considered by critics as perfect craftsmanship. She never wavered from the part
assigned to her by the playwright. For the creation of her role and her
husband's, alone, Frank Wilson deserves much credit. He has done a credit-
able piece of work.

> Frederick W. Bond, "Recent Drama of Negro Authorship," *The Negro and the Drama*
> (1940; rpt. Washington, DC: McGrath, 1969), pp. 109–10

DORIS E. ABRAMSON   Although it was as *Meek Mose* that Frank
Wilson's play was initially produced on Broadway, it was revived in 1934
as *Brother Mose*, described by the Federal Theatre as a three-act "social
drama about the struggles of a Negro group against adverse living conditions
in a small Southern community." This description might lead one to believe
that it was a play of social significance. It was not. Its hero, Brother Mose,
a religious leader who tries to get Negroes to live in accordance with the
tenets of his faith, is related to the hero of Garland Anderson's *Appearances*
or even to Mrs. Stowe's Uncle Tom.

Interestingly enough, although the Federal Theatre called *Brother Mose*
a social drama, the title page of the prompt copy used by the Federal Theatre
Project has on it the subtitle *A Comedy of Negro Life with Music and Spirituals*.
At the front of this typescript appears the statement: "A Negro play, showing
the efficacy of prayer and optimism." This is the version produced by the
Negro units of the Federal Theatre and, presumably, the one used for the
1934 Broadway production.

Even though the characters in *Brother Mose* are specifically described in
terms of lighter and darker complexions and the texture of their hair, there
seems to be no distorted use of this kind of characterization. In other words,
there is no suggestion that either light or dark is superior. The playwright
seems simply to want a representative group of Negroes, light and dark,
young and old, plain and fancy. There are twenty characters, plus a crowd,
and only one white character, a police officer. Whether or not the playwright
addressed himself to any problems of the thirties in the script of his play,
he solved the problem of unemployment for Negro actors by providing them
with roles. ⟨. . .⟩

Songs and dances frequently interrupt the action of the play. In the first
scene of the second act, some of Enos Greene's followers gather around for

a good time. One has a guitar; another, a jew's harp. A song follows. The stage directions then indicate a dance called a Boston, more choruses of the song, a rendition of "Shortenin' Bread," more singing and clowning. Certainly this is a minstrel turn in the midst of what has been described as social drama. ⟨. . .⟩

Though the critics were kind in 1928 and in 1934, Brooks Atkinson recorded reactions to *Meek Mose* that, unfortunately, seem to hold true for the latter *Brother Mose* too:

> With all the good-will in the world toward a Negro theatre as a necessity both of the drama and of contemporary life, it is difficult to record *Meek Mose* as anything better than a childishly naive endeavor, full of sepia tint John Golden and depicting life only in slightly shopworn terms of the theatre. . . . The Negro, in writing about himself, sees himself not as he is, or even approximately, as he is, but in the vivid reds, blues, and greens of the comic strip, becomes, in brief, a caricature and such a caricature as even few whites make him out to be.

Frank Wilson was certainly perpetuating stereotypes. His experience in the theatre may have taught him the necessity of doing so, but as Fannin Belcher observed, "Had the playwright been more interested in interpreting Negro life than in making a show, there might have been less of the minstrel aroma in dialogue and characters."

Doris E. Abramson, *Negro Playwrights in the American Theatre 1925–1959* (New York: Colombia University Press, 1967), pp. 55–59

LOFTEN MITCHELL   The Negro Unit of the Federal Theatre was part of the Works Progress Administration, referred to by many today as the "Grand-daddy of the Anti-Poverty Program." Federal funds were poured into various theatre groups, and actors found employment during the difficult depression years. One such group was the Negro Unit, housed at Harlem's Lafayette.

In 1936 this unit presented Frank Wilson's *Walk Together, Children*, a fine folk drama. Like other ventures that followed, it was seen by audiences for as little as twenty-five cents or by showing a card from the Department of Welfare. ⟨. . .⟩

A note should be made here regarding attendance at the Lafayette. *Walk Together, Children*, which opened February 4, 1936, was seen by 10,530 people. *The Conjure Man Dies*, also produced in 1936, drew 11,100 people. When one realizes these plays were not put on for long runs, one gets an interesting answer to the oft-quoted cliché about Negroes not supporting theatre.

> Loften Mitchell, "The Depression Years: Propaganda Plays, the Federal Theatre, Efforts Toward a New Harlem Theatre," *Black Drama: The Story of the American Negro in the Theatre* (New York: Hawthorne Books, 1967), pp. 100, 102

DARWIN T. TURNER   ⟨. . .⟩ Frank Wilson, an actor, created an unusual protagonist in *Meek Mose*, which opened February 6, 1928. Most black playwrights have refused to write about docile blacks or have portrayed them as villains who must either be converted to self-respect or destroyed before the final curtain. Frank Wilson, however, not only made such a character a protagonist but even rewarded him. When white community leaders propose to move the blacks to a different section of town, peace-loving Mose, a leader of the black community, advises the blacks to agree. The blacks turn on him when disease and death result from the new living conditions, but he is rewarded for his faith when oil is discovered on the new property. Historically, of course, *Meek Mose* retells the success of some American Indians who, driven from their fertile farmland in the East, were forced to relocate in Oklahoma, where oil was later discovered. Nevertheless, it is an unusual theme for a black playwright.

> Darwin T. Turner, "Introduction," *Black Drama: An Anthology*, ed. William Brasmer and Dominick Consolo (Columbus, OH: Charles E. Merrill, 1970), p. 6

▣ *Bibliography*

Published Plays:

Sugar Cain. Opportunity, June 1926. In *Plays of Negro Life*, ed. Alain Locke
    and Montgomery Gregory (1927) (as *Sugar Cane*).
Meek Mose. 1928 (produced), 1937 (as *Brother Mose*).

Plays Written and/or Produced But Not Published::

Back Home Again. 1914–23.

Colored Americans. 1914–23.

Confidence. 1914–20.

The Flash. 1914–23.

The Frisco Kid. 1914–23.

The Good Sister Jones. 1914–23.

Happy Southern Folks. 1914–23.

The Prison Life. 1914–23.

Race Pride. 1914–23.

Roseanna. 1914–23.

Deep Purple. 1917.

The Heartbreaker. 1921.

A Train North. 1923.

Pa Williams' Gal. 1923.

Color Worship. 1926.

Flies. 1926.

The Wall Between. 1929.

Walk Together Chillun. 1936.

Screenplays:

Paradise in Harlem. 1939.

Murder on Lenox Avenue. 1941.

Sunday Sinners. 1941.